**DATE DUE**

| | | | |
|---|---|---|---|
| MR 2 9 '93 | | | |
| APR 1 2 1993 | | | |
| APR 2 8 1993 | | | |
| MAR 3 1 1994 | | | |
| MAR 0 1 1995 | | | |
| MAR 0 9 1995 | | | |
| APR 2 5 1995 | | | |
| MAR 1 0 1997 | | | |
| MY 07 '02 | | | |
| FE 0 4 '04 | | | |
| 5-24-10 | | | |
| | | | |

# TEENAGE DEPRESSION

*Also by Herma Silverstein*


SPIES AMONG US:
The Truth About Modern Espionage

TEEN GUIDE TO
SINGLE PARENTING

# TEENAGE DEPRESSION

## BY HERMA SILVERSTEIN

FRANKLIN WATTS
NEW YORK/LONDON/TORONTO/SYDNEY/1990

Library of Congress Cataloging-in-Publication Data

Silverstein, Herma.
Teenage depression / by Herma Silverstein.
p.    cm.
Includes bibliographical references.
Summary: Explains the different forms of depression due to
environment, chemical imbalance, or genetics, and indicates remedies
or agencies that can help.
ISBN 0-531-15183-2—ISBN 0-531-10960-7
1. Depression in adolescence—Juvenile literature.
[1. Depression, Mental.]   I. Title.
RJ506.D4S56     1990
616.85'27'00835—dc20     90-32997   CIP   AC

# CONTENTS

# TEENAGE DEPRESSION

# 1
# WHAT IS DEPRESSION?

*"Why live? Why die? To keep on living an empty life
takes patience from an empty person. . . ."*

—*from* Vivienne: The Life and Suicide
of an Adolescent Girl

These words are from the diary of Vivienne Loomis, a bright, attractive, well-liked fourteen-year-old who committed suicide in 1973, to the shock of her family and friends. Yet for months, Vivienne had given warning signals that she was depressed. She had confided in her close friends. She had written letters to her teachers. Her cries for help, however, were thought to be merely the typical mood swings of adolescence.[1]

Robert, seventeen, was also bright, attractive, and well-liked. He played quarterback on his high school football team, was voted vice-president of his senior class, maintained a B average, went steady with one of the most popular girls in school, and had a good relationship with his parents. He had recently been accepted by the college of his choice.

But all was not as well as it seemed in Robert's life. Usually outgoing, suddenly Robert became a hermit, staying in his room for hours at a time. He stopped phoning his girlfriend, and refused to talk with her when she phoned him. Where once he got along with his parents, Robert now argued with them, making sarcastic remarks at whatever they said. He quit studying, and received his first grade lower than a B ever—a C on a math quiz.

Then Robert dropped off the football team and stopped doing the activities he once enjoyed, especially surfing, which used to fill almost all his free time. Previously a teenager with a healthy appetite, Robert picked at his food and lost over ten pounds in a month. When his parents pressed him for a reason for his changed behavior, Robert told them, "I just feel down. Like I'm all empty inside."

Robert couldn't understand why he felt so "bummed out" all the time. His friends sometimes felt down, but they always snapped out of it. Maybe he was going crazy. He could not seem to make the simplest decision anymore, such as whether to wear a blue T-shirt or a white one, whether to wear his cord pants or his jeans.

At first his parents thought Robert was just going through a period of normal adolescent blues and would eventually grow out of his moodiness. Weeks later, however, it was clear that Robert's depression had grown worse. Most days he cut school and lay in bed listening to sad music. He complained that life wasn't worth living and talked about "ending it all."

Now frightened, Robert's parents persuaded him to see their family doctor. When she could find no physical reason for Robert's low mood, she suggested he might be suffering from a depressive illness. A psychiatrist confirmed the diagnosis, and Robert began meeting with the psychiatrist once a week. Together they talked about Robert's sad, hopeless feelings, when his depression had started, how it had gotten worse, and how Robert could work toward lifting his overwhelming sadness and begin believing life was worth living again. The psychiatrist also put Robert on an antidepressant medication.

Within six months, Robert's appetite had returned to normal and he was able to concentrate on his schoolwork. Although he occasionally fell into a down mood, the mood was not as paralyzing as before, and lasted only a week at most, instead of going on for months. Within a year, Robert's depression had lifted to the point where he actually felt happy. As he again made plans for college, Robert couldn't believe he had ever wanted to kill himself.

Vivienne and Robert. Two teenagers suffering from the same illness, but with two different outcomes.

Depression such as Robert's and Vivienne's is a severe, debilitating illness. It is unpredictable as to when and at what age it strikes; what, if anything, causes depressive illness to occur; when it will go away; and when, if at all, the illness will return. That is the bad news. The good news is that depression can be treated. And if treated properly, the recurrence is usually less severe and ends sooner.

Depressive illness has been known since biblical times. The Old Testament makes many references to depression and manic-depression (alternating periods of depression and elated, "high" moods) as afflictions of the mind. The word depression comes from the Latin word *deprimere* (to press down). Thus depression has evolved to mean a pressed down, or sad, feeling.

In the fourth century B.C., the Greek physician Hippocrates wrote the first medical description of the disease, which he called *melancholia*, from the Greek word meaning "a mental disorder involving prolonged fear and depression." Hippocrates described a woman "of melancholic turn of mind, from some accidental cause of sorrow [who] while still going about became affected with loss of sleep, aversion to food and had thirst and nausea."[2] He also described an illness with elated, overly excited symptoms which he called *mania*. However, he saw no connection between the two conditions.[3]

In the medieval humoral theory of medicine, four humors, or body fluids, were believed to determine a person's temperament. These fluids were blood (the sanguine or cheerful personality), phlegm (the phlegmatic or nonemotional personality), yellow bile (the choleric or hot-tempered personality), and black

11

bile (the melancholic or depressed personality). Since black bile was thought to cause depressive disorders, these illnesses came to be called "melancholic diseases."[4]

In the late Middle Ages, religious leaders believed depression was caused by possession of evil spirits. The German religious reformer Martin Luther wrote: "All heaviness of mind and melancholy comes of the Devil."[5] Through the years, depression has been treated with such remedies as whipping, bloodletting, exorcism, and soothing baths.

In 1864, the French psychiatrist Falret noticed that some of his depressed patients went through periods of over-excitement and agitation characteristic of mania, then fell into deep depression. Thus he realized that the two separate conditions described by Hippocrates could, in some patients, actually be one illness characterized by alternating periods of depression and mania. Falret had essentially discovered a new type of depressive illness, which he named *folie circulaire* (circular madness), today called "manic-depressive illness."

At that time, "folie circulaire" was considered a form of schizophrenia (a chronic, or ongoing, illness characterized by bizarre thoughts, in which the person loses all sense of reality). Then in 1896, the German psychiatrist Emil Kraepelin discovered that schizophrenia and manic-depressive illness were two different mental illnesses. Kraepelin observed that schizophrenia eventually caused mental deterioration, while manic-depressive disease did not. Manic-depressive patients went through periods of illness alternating with long periods of health.

Further, Kraepelin distinguished manic-depressive illness from the illness of depression only. As a result of Kraepelin's discoveries, some form of the word "depression" replaced the word melancholia as the diagnostic term for depressive illness.[6]

Because talking to a psychiatrist made some depressed people feel better, in the early 1900s depression was believed to be caused by psychological traumas. The physician Alexander Haig wrote in 1900: "In this condition self-reliance is absolutely gone . . . a feather weight will crush one to the dust, and even the greatest good fortune will fail to cheer."[7]

By the 1960s, antidepressant medications were discovered that relieved depression by correcting chemical imbalances in the brain. Thus many scientists and doctors came to believe that neurochemical imbalances caused depression, rather than psychological traumas.

It has never been proven beyond a doubt whether depression is primarily caused by biological or psychological reasons. Most experts now believe depression is caused by a combination of the two.

Today depression and manic-depression are among the most common disorders in psychiatry. Six to seven percent of adolescents suffer from depressive illness.[8] One study estimates that 1.8 percent (approximately 400,000) of the children in the 7-to-12-year-old age group suffer severe depression.[9] One woman in five and one man in ten can expect to develop a depressive or manic-depressive episode at least once in their lives.

Yet according to the National Institute of Mental Health (NIMH) in Bethesda, Maryland, only 30 percent of depressed people seek any type of professional help. One reason is that many people do not want to believe they have a mental illness. Another reason is that most nonpsychiatric doctors focus on physical symptoms instead of emotional symptoms in diagnosing illnesses, and fail to consider depression as the cause of their patients' complaints. One study found that one-half to three-quarters of nonpsychiatric medical doctors fail to diagnose depressive illness in patients who later were found to have the illness.[10]

Therefore, NIMH started a Depression Awareness, Recognition and Treatment program (DART) aimed at alerting nonpsychiatric doctors to the possibility of depression as a diagnosis when no physical cause could be found to explain a patient's symptoms.[11]

The word "mood" in medical terminology is also referred to as "affect," or the way people look and carry themselves. Depressed affects, for example, include a slumped posture and a slow walk. Manic affects include agitated movements, fast walking, and pacing back and forth.[12]

Because depression changes a person's affect, depressive illnesses are often referred to as "affective disorders." In contrast to psychotic illnesses in which a person suffers increasing unawareness of reality, affective disorders usually occur as one episode, or attack, after which the illness goes into remission for a period of time.

Some people, however, do become so severely depressed that they cannot function. These people need to be hospitalized to get proper treatment. Other people are less physically and socially paralyzed. This second group often experiences depression as sadness, lack of energy, and feelings of failure. These symptoms may last for weeks or months, regardless of what else is going on in the person's life.

Depression is nonprejudiced in the people it strikes: young or old, famous or unknown, rich, middle class, or homeless. Some of the more well-known people who have suffered from depression include the Bible's King Saul, Queen Elizabeth I, President Abraham Lincoln, author Ernest Hemingway, former First Lady Betty Ford, and the late British Prime Minister Winston Churchill, who called depression "the black dog that shadowed my life." [13]

Whether in a child, a teenager, or an adult, true depressive illness is different from feeling sad or lonely after a traumatic event or change in life occurs, such as the death of a relative or pet, a parents' divorce, moving to a new city or school, or breaking up with a boy- or girlfriend. For underneath this type of sadness is a feeling of hope that eventually the depression will go away, and life will again be happier.

Although depression that occurs after a traumatic event may make people lose their desire to perform daily routines, somehow they manage to continue to function. For example, a teenager may not want to go to school, but that teenager does go to school. His or her assignments may not be up to usual standards, but he or she still makes an effort to turn in the homework. After a time of grieving and adjustment, these people's sadness disappears, and they go on with their lives. The teenager starts to find it less difficult to study, and once again looks forward to the activities enjoyed before.

True depressive illness is also different from the "blues" that adolescents normally experience due to hormonal changes in their bodies. Adolescent blues are short-lived and can be instantly relieved by something happy or exciting occurring. On the other hand, teenagers with true depressive illness continue to feel sad, sometimes for months, no matter what happy or exciting events occur in their lives. A truly depressed teenager could be given a car of his or her choice and still feel sad.

If untreated, the sadness of depressive illness grows so strong that people feel helpless and hopeless, as if their world has caved in on them, and there is nothing they or anyone else can do to get them out of the ruins and make them happy again. In fact, truly depressed people believe that things will only get worse, never better.

In some cases, their depression is so severe that any normal activity, such as getting out of bed, eating, or even talking, requires enormous energy. Eventually, these individuals have no desire to do anything, neither the fun activities they used to enjoy, nor being with people they care about. Some severely depressed people cannot function at all. They stay in bed or sit in a chair all day, staring at the walls.

The three major clues in determining whether you have a normal case of "the blues," or a true depressive illness, are the length of time you have felt depressed, the severity of the depression (feeling helpless and hopeless), and whether the depression affects your daily routine. A fourth clue, and an important one, is that people with depressive illness can feel extremely sad for no reason at all.

Until the 1980s, psychiatrists did not believe that children and teenagers could suffer from depression. They believed that true depression could not exist before the development of a person's idealized self-image (called the superego), which usually did not occur until late adolescence. Now, however, according to a report from the National Institute of Mental Health, it is known that between three and six million American children suffer from depression.[14] In fact, one-fourth of hospitalized manic-depressive patients experienced their first depressive or manic episode between the ages of ten and nineteen.[15]

It has even been discovered that infants can suffer severe depression, called a "reactive attachment disorder," because the baby is reacting to a lack of adequate attention and nurturing, especially from the mother. These infants do not show appropriate responses to stimuli, such as following movements with their eyes or smiling when they see their parents' faces or hear their voices.[16]

Most teenagers diagnosed as having depressive illness also have school difficulties, such as academic failure, truancy, and behavioral problems. Although symptoms of depression in teenagers are similar to those in adults, many times the illness goes unrecognized by parents, and therefore remains untreated. One reason is that during adolescence, it is common for teenagers' moods to dramatically swing up and down. The difference is that a truly depressed teenager has no hope of feeling better, and happy events in their lives do not lift them out of depression.

Most of these teenagers know they feel abnormally sad, but they do not know that what they are feeling is a symptom of an illness, not merely a down mood. If they never learn that what they are experiencing is a treatable illness, they begin to feel they must be crazy. Why else, they ask themselves, do they feel so miserable for no reason?

Kay, a fifteen-year-old said,

> Until I was about fourteen, I wanted to do, see, and be everything. I was on the tennis team at school, the city gymnastics team, dove off the high board the first time I climbed the ladder, had a ton of friends, and even made good grades. Then one morning I woke up all sad inside. It was a drag just to get out of bed. The sad feeling got worse, and I'd cry for no reason.
> Pretty soon I was walking around like a zombie,

not caring whether my friends phoned, if I failed a test, lost a tennis match, flubbed a balance beam routine, what was for dinner, or even if there was dinner. Sometimes I just went to sleep as soon as I got home from school and didn't get up again until the next morning.

On the other hand, some teenagers, not knowing the difference between the normal feelings of being down and true depression, assume everyone feels as they do. Jeff, sixteen, said, "As far back as I can remember, I'd wake up every morning wanting to cry. I thought everyone woke up feeling sad, like their mother or father had died. When I finally got so depressed I couldn't get out of bed, I thought I'd lost it. My folks took me to a psychiatrist. That was a real trip. And I don't mean the ride in the car. I mean finding out I had an illness that makes people sad, and I wasn't crazy after all."

Parents who do not know that depression can be an illness rationalize their youngster's depressive symptoms as either crankiness in the younger child or normal rebellion in the teenager. If left untreated, depression in young people can result in learning problems, school failure, drug and alcohol abuse, disturbed relationships with other people, criminal activities, suicide, and even homicide.

The major symptoms of teenage depression are:

1. *A feeling of sadness and hopelessness.* Depressed teenagers believe there is no way to stop feeling stressed out and sad.
2. *Moodiness.* Depressed teenagers experience alternating feelings of anger and sadness for weeks at a time.
3. *Eating disturbances.* Depressed teenagers either eat too much or too little, and the change from their normal eating habits continues for a long time.
4. *Sleep disturbances.* Nightmares are common, as is difficulty falling asleep, or awakening early, due to the stress of all the anxieties they feel.

5. *Changes in social life.* Depressed teenagers stop spending time with friends. They often refuse phone calls.
6. *Chemical abuse.* Depressed teenagers abuse drugs and alcohol to relieve depression, but often the result is that they become "hooked" on drugs. Because alcohol and drugs are depressants, not mood elevators, the teenager's depression worsens.
7. *Loss of interest in pleasurable activities.* Depressed teenagers find no pleasure in activities they used to enjoy, such as going to movies or rock concerts, reading books, watching television, listening to music, or participating in sports. Neither do they get involved in new activities.
8. *Suicidal ideas.* Depressed teenagers become obsessed with death, and some actually kill themselves.[17]

To be diagnosed as having a depressive illness, you must have experienced for at least two weeks, at least four of the following symptoms listed in the American Psychiatric Association's *Diagnostic and Statistical Manual of Mental Disorders,* 3rd Edition (the DSM III):

1. poor appetite or significant weight loss (when not dieting) or increased appetite or significant weight gain,
2. insomnia or . . . excessive sleeping,
3. psychomotor agitation or retardation (slowness),
4. loss of interest or pleasure in usual activities, or decrease in sexual drive,
5. loss of energy; fatigue,
6. feelings of worthlessness, self-reproach, or excessive or inappropriate guilt,
7. diminished ability to think or concentrate, such as slowed thinking, or indecisiveness (unable to make simple decisions, such as what to wear to school or eat for breakfast),
8. recurrent thoughts of death . . . wishes to be dead, or suicide attempts[18]

Further, the eight symptoms listed above cannot have occurred as a result of an organic illness, such as influenza, hypothyroidism, cancer, Alzheimer's disease, or other brain diseases leading to mental deterioration. Neither can the symptoms be the result of grief due to the death of a close relative or friend.[19]

The DSM III diagnostic manual is a general outline of depressive illness symptoms. Some symptoms may require further explanation.

Slowed thinking occurs when depressed people cannot handle ordinary amounts of information. For example, in English class, the teacher talks about only one play by Shakespeare, but the depressed student feels overwhelmed by facts, as if the teacher is giving an entire course on Shakespearean plays in one hour. As a result, the person lives in a constant state of mental confusion.

Bouts of crying for no reason are another common symptom. Some depressed people, however, complain of the inability to cry, even though they feel tearful. These people say being unable to cry, a way to let out some of their sad feelings, is far more painful than being racked by sobs for hours at a time.

There are several special symptoms of depression which, although they do not occur in half the diagnosed cases, are nevertheless not rare, and are also important indicators of depressive illness. One, called "diurnal variation," is a change in mood as the day wears on. A person wakes up in the morning feeling sad and having trouble concentrating. Then as the day progresses, the person feels more normal, and by evening feels almost nondepressed.

Kelly, seventeen, is a typical example of this type of depressive. An accomplished pianist, her goal was to become a concert pianist. When she was fifteen, however, she lost almost all her interest in the piano. She would awake each morning filled with a feeling of gloom. By midafternoon she would feel a little of her old joy in playing the piano. By dinnertime, she was almost, but not quite, lost in the feeling of accomplishment her practice used to give her.

19

She would do her homework and fall asleep easily. After about three hours, however, she would awake slightly depressed, and fight to get back to sleep. Around five o'clock in the morning, Kelly would wake up severely depressed, unable to fall asleep again. By the time her alarm went off, her depression had returned to a severe state.

About one-third of depressed people suffer from anxiety attacks. These attacks usually disappear when the depression lifts. An anxiety attack is a feeling of intense fear for no apparent reason. The person feels impending doom, as if he or she were nailed to railroad tracks with a speeding locomotive careening toward him or her. A series of physical symptoms usually accompany anxiety attacks, such as heart palpitations, dizziness, sweating, chest pains, and shortness of breath.

If you experience an anxiety attack and cannot catch your breath, the tendency is to gasp for air. But this will only make you dizzy, and you may faint. If you are at home, put a small paper bag over your nose and mouth and breathe into it for a few minutes. You will be breathing out carbon dioxide and then reinhaling it, which will slow your breathing back to normal. If you do not have a paper bag, cup your hands around your nose and mouth and breathe into your palms.

Feelings of guilt also occur in a third of depressed people. Often patients think back over the years and focus on one failure or minor mistake. Or they apologize for mistakes that were not their fault. They feel they should expect punishment for these imagined mistakes or failures.

One thirty-year-old depressed man recalled that when he was a senior in high school, he had cheated on a math test. Now a successful accountant, he had not thought of the incident until depression struck, then he was unable to think of anything else.

Some patients develop delusions, or false ideas, of a depressive nature. A teenager will believe her parents are spying on her, listening in on her phone calls, or reading her mail. Often the teenager feels guilt along with the delusion. She feels she has done something awful, and her parents need to spy on her to make sure she does not do this terrible thing again.[20]

Another symptom of depression is mania, which is actually part of a specific type of depression called "manic-depressive illness." (This will be dealt with fully in Chapter Four.) Mania shows up as either an extremely elated mood (euphoric) or an extremely irritable mood. It has been estimated that there are ten patients who suffer depression for every one patient who suffers manic-depression.[21]

When people suffer severe depression, hopelessness turns to despair, and despair to desperation. In a panic, they latch onto anything they think will give them relief from the painful sadness inside them. Many teenagers turn to alcohol and drugs. While these forms of "self-medication" may give them some temporary relief from depression, the relief does not last. In fact, such chemical abuse actually causes the depression to return with greater force.

The most tragic consequence of depression is suicide. This last resort is sometimes the result of such low self-esteem that the teenager feels his or her life is not worth living and everyone around would be better off if he or she were dead (another form of delusion). Other times, suicide is the result of overdosing on alcohol or drugs.

Today depressive illness is no longer seen as a hopeless mental illness, with the patient's future a clouded window. With more and more research being conducted into the illness of depression, streams of sunlight are shining through those clouded windows, brightening the moods of depressed people by shedding new light into the causes of this illness of despair.

# 2
# THE CAUSES OF DEPRESSION: PSYCHOLOGICAL, GENETIC, AND ENVIRONMENTAL

*"I am now the most miserable man living. If what I feel were equally distributed to the whole human family, there would not be one cheerful face on earth. . . ."*

*—Abraham Lincoln*

Depression is a "family affair," says Professor Myrna Weissman, director of Yale University's depression research unit. "If one parent is depressed, the likelihood of their children becoming depressed increases two- to threefold. If both parents are depressed, the chances are increased four- to sixfold."[1] One study suggests a child has a 30 percent chance of showing signs of depression by age six or seven if the mother has depressive illness, and a 50 percent chance if both parents are depressed.[2] An estimated two-thirds of relatives of depressed patients also have been depressed.[3]

Samuel Johnson (1709–1784), the English biographer and author of a notable English dictionary, said, "I inherited a vile melancholy from my father, which has made me mad all my life. . . ." Other biographers have written of family histories of depressive illness. The English poet Byron, German composer Robert Schumann, and American statesman Robert E. Lee, in addition to being afflicted themselves, all had depressed relatives.

Although depressive illness has been known for hundreds of

years to run in families, until the 1960s scientists had no way of telling whether children became depressed because they inherited the disease, or because of their environment—living with a depressed parent or having little nurturing as children from their parents.

Then researchers began studying adopted children, who inherited their genes from their biological parents, and their environment from their adopted parents. If depression is caused by environment, it would be expected that a child born of a depressed parent would not be depressed if adopted and raised by nondepressed parents. But if depression is genetically passed from parent to child, then adopted children would have just as great a chance of becoming depressed whether raised by biological or adoptive parents.

Studies of adopted children whose biological parents had depressive illness or manic-depressive illness found these children had a greater tendency to develop one of these illnesses than did children whose biological parents were not depressed.[4]

However, depression can skip generations. A grandparent may have depressive illness, while his or her children will not inherit the disease, but the grandchildren will. The type and severity of depressive illness can also vary from one generation to another. For example, a parent can be manic-depressive, and the child can have mild depression with no manic stage, or severe depression.[5]

Studies of twins have also shown compelling evidence that depression is a genetic illness. Researchers have discovered the same type of depression in pairs of identical twins who were raised by different adoptive parents. If one identical twin suffers from depression, the likelihood that the other will, too, is between 40 and 70 percent, whether the twins are raised together or apart. For nonidentical twins, the likelihood is zero to 13 percent.[6]

In 1987, researchers from the Massachusetts Institute of Technology, the Miami School of Medicine, and Yale University School of Medicine, working with the Amish population, found a gene on chromosome 11 that triggers manic-depression in 60 to 70 percent of people who inherit this gene, again confirming the theory of inheritance as a cause for depression.[7] And University of Rochester geneticist, Dr. Lowell R. Weitkamp, working with University of Toronto psychiatrist Harvey C. Stancer, found that in families with two depressed children, the depressed siblings tended to share a type of human leucocyte antigen (HLA). An antigen is an enzyme that causes an immune (disease-fighting) reaction in the body, and leucocytes are the white matter in the brain.

Although many scientists believe the HLA theory needs more study before it can be considered diagnostically accurate, Drs. Weitkamp and Stancer believe their test means that the genes predisposing (making it possible for) people to become depressed are physically linked to the HLA antigens.[8] If a genetic marker can be proven beyond a doubt to cause depression, then a lab test can show who has the disease and who does not.

Psychopharmacologists, scientists who study drugs and their effects, are trying to isolate the exact role of different neurochemicals in different types of depression, and then develop a drug for each type. By testing blood, spinal fluid, and urine, they have uncovered differences in the ratios of certain chemicals in the bodies of depressed people. For example, a manic-depressive patient's biochemistry differs in specific ways from a patient suffering from depression only.[9]

What is inherited in depression is a chemical imbalance in the brain. The brain contains billions of nerve cells that form a communications network for relaying messages from one cell to another. These messages are transmitted by chemicals called neurotransmitters. Studies have revealed that depressed people have imbalances in the amounts of neurotransmitters thought to play a major role in the regulation of emotions, especially the neurotransmitters norepinephrine, serotonin, and dopamine.[10]

Norepinephrine and serotonin dispatch messages vital to such basic functions as sleep, appetite, concentration, and sex, as well as to emotions like happiness, sadness, and even the will to live. According to William Potter, a chief of clinical pharmacology at NIMH, people with either depressive illness or manic-depressive illness react with an overrelease of norepinephrine when stressed. Moreover, he says, all antidepressant drugs eventually affect the norepinephrine system.[11]

"Norepinephrine is a device for focusing in on stimuli from the environment," Dr. Potter says. "The depressed person suffers from characteristic distortions—for example, seeing criticism where there is none—because he's unable to take in and process information correctly."[12]

Besides genetic origins of depression, there are psychological reasons that, either acting alone cause a person to become depressed, or cause depression when activated in the form of stress in a person who is genetically predisposed to depressive illness.

A teenager with a family history of depression who is not depressed herself is suddenly faced with the death of her mother. Naturally she is depressed over her mother's death. But her depression worsens over time instead of getting better. "Grief has triggered a biochemical depression in an inherently vulnerable person,"[13] says Dr. John Mann, director of laboratory psychopharmacology at Cornell Medical College.

Stress experiments have revealed strong connections between depression and anxiety. Says Aaron Beck, a professor of psychiatry at the University of Pennsylvania, "An anxious person *fears* things won't turn out, a depressed person *believes* they won't."[14] Many depressed people are anxious as well as depressed. Some anxiety disorders, such as agoraphobia (fear of open spaces), are now being successfully treated with antidepressants, which implies that the same neurochemicals are involved in both anxiety and depression.

The main psychological cause of depression is attachment and loss. Whenever we become attached to a person, place, thing, or state of well being, we also risk losing that person, place, thing, or state of well being. Children who are moved from foster home to foster home will no longer attach to adults. They have learned that attaching results in being rejected (loss). Therefore, these children refuse to risk loss anymore. From 26 to 30 percent of depressed people, including teenagers and children, develop a severe depressive illness following a loss—of a job, the death of a loved one, a divorce, a separation, the breakup of a relationship, moving to a new home or school, losing an athletic event, and even failing a test in school.

People who develop depressive illness due to loss seem to have less ability to cope with stress than people who overcome their losses in time.[15]

Another cause of depression is a childhood trauma, such as being abused or sexually molested by a parent. The psychoanalytic theory of depression claims these children repress, or lock away, the traumas in the subconscious part of their minds. However, although the childhood event is repressed, the accompanying emotions are not. Thus these children feel a sense of sadness, helplessness, guilt, fear, or anger that they believe is for no reason.

Later in life, when an event occurs that is similar to the childhood trauma, these same feelings of depression reemerge. Usually, without the help of psychotherapy, the childhood incident remains forgotten, and these people fail to recognize the connection between the current unhappy experience and the childhood one. They do not understand why they always feel depressed, or why their depression lingers long after a loss, when most people would have started feeling better.

Other experts believe that when children and teenagers who have inherited the tendency to become depressed experience a childhood trauma, the trauma triggers the depression. Without the trauma, researchers believe, these people would never become depressed.

Other doctors believe the event that triggers the depression does not have to be traumatic when the tendency to become depressed is inherited. As proof, they cite the fact that such teenagers get depressed simply because their parents do not pay enough attention to them. In addition, children and teenagers without a predisposition to depression can experience abuse and even abandonment without getting depressed.[16]

Destructive relationships within the family can also trigger depression in teenagers. At great risk for depression are adolescents whose parents are abusive, overly critical of their child's inadequacies, have too high expectations, or who show a lack of care and attention.

Depression is also common in teenagers whose parents do not allow them to express negative feelings, or who refuse to listen to these negative feelings if the parents do not agree with them. By being listened to, teenagers learn that their parents validate their feelings. Communication with parents is an important "vaccine" for teenage depression.

When parents fail to listen to their teenagers' concerns, put them down, or minimize their problems and feelings, communication is blocked. The teenager feels what he or she says does not matter. In fairness, it must be said that many teenagers also contribute or may even cause the block in communication with their parents by doing the same not-listening, and putting down of the behavior of their parents. A common conversation blocker between parents and teenagers is starting sentences with the expression "The trouble with you is. . . ."

When teenagers' feelings are not respected or treated as real by their parents, teenagers feel guilty about their feelings. And when a real crisis occurs, these teenagers are afraid to talk with their parents, or they assume that talking would be useless, as their parents would again just put down their feelings or become angry at them for having negative feelings.

There are times, however, when teenagers' problems are serious enough that only talking to a psychiatrist or another mental health worker will help. Seeing a psychiatrist does not mean that you are a failure or are mentally ill. Psychiatrists who work with teenagers do so because they have a sincere interest in helping them solve their problems and develop into healthy adults. Psychiatrists care about their patients, and do not consider them "crazy," but rather consider them people who have real problems that need to be worked out in order for them to go on with their lives.

Depression can also occur in children and teenagers who are forced to grow up too quickly, either because of a family crisis in which adult responsibilities are forced upon them at too early an age, or because parents have unreasonably high expectations of them. Teenagers become depressed when they know they can never meet their parents' high expectations.

An average female student has no interest in a professional career that requires a college education. After graduating from high school, she wants to attend a vocational school, where she can learn to be a beautician, or learn about carpentry or cooking. Her parents, however, have always dreamed of her becoming a lawyer. They insist she attend college. She follows their wishes and tries to make good grades, but fails, bringing on a hopeless feeling that leads to depression.[17]

Recent studies of infant mental development have led scientists to conclude that babies' brains are far more sophisticated than previously thought, and may be emotionally influenced by prenatal (in the womb) experiences. Depression in the mother could be passed on to the fetus in the womb. According to Dr. Thomas Verny, coauthor of *The Secret Life of the Unborn Child,* from the sixth month of pregnancy on, the embryo can already remember, hear, feel, and even learn; by the seventh to eighth month, the fetal brain's neural circuits are just as advanced as a newborn's. Thus, Dr. Verny claims, mother-infant bonding (attachment) actually begins in the womb.

Dr. Verny explains his theory with the fact that intense, prolonged anxiety during pregnancy can increase a mother's output of neurohormones (hormones produced by the brain) into her bloodstream. Whatever goes into the mother's bloodstream also goes into the fetus's. Therefore, these hormones not only alter the mother's body chemistry but that of her unborn child's as well, possibly raising the child's susceptibility to emotional distress.

"You can see the aftereffects of this in a nonemotional newborn or a distracted sixteen-year-old; for emotional patterns set in the womb may plague a child for the rest of his or her life," says Dr. Verny. "That's why treating infant depression has recently become one of psychiatry's leading priorities."[18]

Many parents do not intentionally abuse their children. However, when parents themselves are depressed, they are barely able to take care of their own needs, much less the needs of their children. They may not realize that their child's depression is not normal, since they themselves were depressed as kids, and they believe that unexplained, deep sadness is a normal mood state.

Teenagers experience countless hormonal changes, which make them focus on themselves and their feelings, rather than on what is happening in their parents' lives. Therefore, many teenagers mistakenly view their parents' withdrawal of attention and affection, or sudden angry, impatient, and critical attitudes toward them as a fault in themselves, rather than as symptoms of their parents' depressive illness. These teenagers may try anything to please their parents, not realizing that nothing is going to please them until their parents get treatment for their own depression.

Some scientists believe depression can be a learned emotion. This "cognitive theory" maintains that children with depressed parents, not knowing differently, view their parents' behavior as normal and copy their parents' depressed behavior. These children learn to be depressed.

In "learned helplessness" experiments, animals that are unable to avoid electric shocks become depressed-looking and undergo changes in their neurochemistry. Later, when given an opportunity to avoid the shocks, they don't even try. On the other hand, animals who can initially avoid the shocks do not show the depressed moods.

From such experiments researchers propose a scenario for depression that seemingly has no cause: Major stress, such as lack of parental love and care, occurs early in a girl's life. This stress is coded in the girl's memory, creating a sensitivity for lack of love. Later, a breakup with her high school boyfriend reactivates that sensitivity, and her first major depressive episode occurs. Later, she may not even require an external stress to become depressed.[19]

Adolescence is a time of accelerated changes in teenagers' bodies and lives. Most teenagers feel unsettled and uncomfortable with these changes. For this reason, teenagers are especially susceptible to depression. Since they experience frequent ups and downs in their moods, it is easy for parents to mistake severe depressive illness for normal adolescent depression. The clues are again the number and severity of symptoms and how long they last. Teenagers who experience four or more symptoms of depression for two weeks or longer should suspect they are suffering from depressive illness, not normal teenage blues.

Adolescence itself is a form of loss—of childhood and the secure feeling of depending on parents to take care of you. By adding other significant losses to loss of childhood, such as changing from the personal, small environment of elementary school to the impersonal, large environment of junior high, teenagers feel even more insecure and uncertain. This sense of loss becomes worse when adults blandly tell teenagers, "Don't worry. You'll get over it." Instead of being comforting, these words make light of the emotional sense of loss. Teenagers may then begin to feel depressed because they feel guilty about having depressed feelings in the first place, and wonder why they can't cope better, and why they aren't "getting over it."

Usually, however, one loss is not enough to bring on a major depression. It is a series of losses or changes that cause the depressive illness. Even positive changes can leave people feeling depressed. For instance, when you achieve a goal, such as finishing high school or getting accepted by your first-choice college, suddenly you get what you have wanted for a long time. The feeling is, for some people, "Now what?" By achieving a goal, you lose it. Achievement is a form of loss for some people.

## MEDICAL TESTS FOR DEPRESSION

Traditionally, diagnosing depressive illness has depended upon observation of the patient's behavior. Now, however, several biological tests have been developed that give psychiatrists ways to be more exact in their diagnosis of depressive illness. Dr. John Rush, director of the Affective Disorders Unit at the University of Texas Medical School in Dallas, says, "Until now, treating depression has been much like treating a swollen ankle without seeing an X ray first to determine whether the problem is a sprain or a broken bone.''[20]

The Dexamethasone Suppression Test (DST) is based on how different levels of neurohormones affect the body. A malfunction in neurohormones can result in stress by causing an imbalance of a hormone in the brain's pituitary gland.

In the Dexamethasone Suppression Test, the patient takes a dose of dexamethasone (usually in pill form), a synthetic version of cortisol. The brain reacts to the dose as if it were an excessive amount of cortisol. In a nondepressed person, the pituitary gland stops its daily secretions of cortisol for at least twenty-four hours, until the cortisol level returns to normal. But in depressed people, the pituitary gland keeps secreting cortisol.

A person usually takes the dexamethasone pill at 11:00 P.M. The next day that person has two blood tests, one at 8:00 A.M. and the other at 4:00 P.M. (Some doctors differ in the hours the blood tests are taken.) How much cortisol is in the blood, according to a predetermined scale, tells whether or not the person is depressed.

Studies have shown that the DST is 50 percent accurate in diagnosing biological depression in adolescents between the ages of twelve and eighteen. In addition, the DST shows the body's response to different antidepressants, thus indicating if a particular antidepressant is working, and shows when the body's neurohormones are rebalanced, thus determining when an antidepressant can be discontinued.[21]

Another test for depression is the Thyroid Hormone Stimulation Test (TRH), which is also used to rule out thyroid disease as the cause of a person's depression.

In the TRH stimulation test, a blood sample is taken to measure the person's regular thyroid-stimulating hormone level. Then the hormone TRH is given to the person. Blood samples are taken at intervals of fifteen, thirty, and ninety minutes to see how much thyroid-stimulating hormones are in the blood. In people without thyroid disease, within an hour there will be modest amounts of thyroid-stimulating hormones above the normal amount, indicating that the depression this person feels is not due to thyroid disease, but rather to depressive illness.

The TRH stimulation test can identify biological depression in about 85 percent of patients with depression.

Another test is the sleep X-ray picture of the brain, called an electroencephalograph (EEG), which diagnoses biological depression by revealing abnormal sleep patterns. Still another test is a urine sample, in which scientists look for the presence of a chemical called PAA that acts as a mood elevator, controlling excitement, wakefulness, and alertness. Depressed people have less PAA in their urine than nondepressed people.[22]

Scientists predict that in the future, biological markers will be found to identify people who are likely to develop an entire range of mental problems, including depression, *before* these problems occur. According to researchers, the future looks promising.

# 3
# TYPES OF DEPRESSIVE ILLNESS

*"Melancholy was made not for beasts but for men;*
*but if men give way to it overmuch*
*they turn to beasts."*

—*Miguel de Cervantes,*
*Spanish novelist*

Carol, sixteen, seemed to have everything going for her—she was a gifted student who breezed through exams as easily as sledding downhill, she was going with the guy she'd been hoping would ask her out since she started high school, she had plenty of friends, and she'd just gotten a great summer job as a day camp counselor. Then one morning Carol woke up anxious for no reason. She felt fidgety and couldn't sit still for more than a few minutes at a time. She couldn't stop her mind at night from churning out thoughts long enough to fall asleep, and she didn't feel like eating. Within a month, Carol lost fifteen pounds.

Dave, fifteen, usually an active teenager, into all types of sports, suddenly started staying home all the time. He lost interest in what his friends were doing. Sometimes he felt so tired that even talking took too much energy.

Beth, eighteen, who normally saved the money she made from her after-school job, only spending when she absolutely had to, such as for Christmas and birthday gifts for her parents and two close friends, suddenly, for no recognizable reason, spent almost three years' worth of savings on trendy clothes.

Although these teenagers' symptoms are different, they are all suffering from depression. Depression wears many faces, has many causes, and can strike anyone at any age, from childhood to old age. Depressive illness, called "Affective Disorders" in the American Psychiatric Association's Diagnostic and Statistical Manual of Mental Disorders, 3rd Edition, (the DSM III), divides Affective Disorders into three classifications:

1. *Major Affective Disorders* (which include "major depression" [unipolar] and "bipolar disorder" [manic-depression])
2. *Other Specific Affective Disorders* (which include "cyclothymic disorder" and "dysthymic disorder")
3. *Atypical Affective Disorders* (which include "atypical bipolar disorder" and "atypical depression").[1]

"Probably the most important thing to remember," says Dr. Frederic Quitkin, head of the Depression Evaluation Service at New York State's Psychiatric Institute, "is that depression occurs on a spectrum, from the ordinary down moods that everyone experiences to the major, crippling kinds of depression that may require hospitalization."[2]

## I. MAJOR AFFECTIVE DISORDERS

According to the DSM III, in order to be diagnosed as having a Major Affective Disorder, you must experience for at least two weeks at least four of the symptoms listed below. The essential symptom of Major Affective Disorder is that the person has suffered either a manic episode or a major depressive episode.

34

## SUBCATEGORIES OF MAJOR
## AFFECTIVE DISORDERS

### A. Major Depression (unipolar)

The essential feature in major depression, also called unipolar depression, is either frequent dysphoric moods (an unbearable feeling of being unhappy) or a loss of interest or pleasure in all or almost all usual activities and pastimes. Normally the symptoms appear over a period of days or weeks, are persistent, and are associated with other symptoms of depressive illness, such as appetite disturbance and feelings of worthlessness.[3]

The illness affects twice as many women as men. A person suffering from a major depressive episode will frequently describe her mood as "not caring anymore." Untreated, a unipolar depressive episode usually lasts from four months to a year. In a lifetime, a person averages five to seven episodes, but as many as forty have been recorded. Some people experience the illness at stressful times; others for no apparent reason.

"It's like having a sword hanging over your head,"[4] says Robert Prien, a National Institute of Mental Health psychologist. Frederick Goodwin, a NIMH scientific director, says, "When the symptoms become the focus of your life, disconnected from what's going on in your environment, that's depression."[5]

Other symptoms associated with major depression include tearfulness, anxiety, irritability, fear, brooding, excessive concern with physical health, panic attacks, and phobias. Sometimes delusions or hallucinations occur, and their content usually depends upon the mood the person is experiencing at the moment. A girl who is feeling fearful might have a delusion that she is being spied upon, or that someone is following her with the intention of hurting her. Or a boy who is feeling guilty may have a delusion that he is being persecuted by his parents because he has committed some imagined sin. Hallucinations are short-lived and may involve voices that put down the person for his faults or alleged sins.[6]

In adolescents, negative or antisocial behavior may appear. Common feelings are wanting to run away from home, not being understood or approved of, restlessness, grouchiness, aggression, sulkiness, a reluctance to participate in family outings, withdrawal from social activities, and retreating into one's room. School difficulties are likely. Depressed teenagers often do not care about their appearance and develop extra sensitivity to rejection in love relationships. Substance abuse is also common.[7]

B. Bipolar Disorder (Manic-Depressive Illness)

Of the nearly fourteen million Americans who have depressive illness, one-third have bipolar disorder. In this illness, a person seesaws between two moods—soaring into an elevated manic mood of either frenzied activity or extreme irritability, and then crashing into depression. One woman recalled that once during her manic stage, she charged $27,000 worth of clothes. She also could not sleep for more than three hours a night.

In the manic state, which lasts at least one week and usually longer, people have extraordinary self-confidence that makes them act recklessly—they will drive a car at breakneck speed, run stoplights, become sexually indiscreet, or go on wild shopping sprees.[8]

Other symptoms of the manic state include nonstop talking, hyperactivity, and behavior the person does not realize is intrusive, demanding, and interfering to other people, such as giving unasked-for opinions or phoning friends at all hours of the night. Although the most typical mood in the manic state is euphoria (cheerfulness), the other typical mood is irritability, in which the person complains, argues, and makes hostile comments.[9]

When not in the manic mood, the person falls into depression, with all the symptoms of major depression. The depressed state may last hours, months, or, more rarely, days. The antidepressant medication lithium is the usual medication prescribed for manic depressive illness.[10] (A more detailed explanation of bipolar disorder is in Chapter Four.)

## II. OTHER SPECIFIC AFFECTIVE DISORDERS

These disorders, which include dysthymic disorder and cyclothymic disorder, usually first appear in adolescence without any reason, but are not severe enough and do not last long enough to meet the criteria for a major depressive or manic episode. The essential feature of other specific affective disorders is a long-lasting disturbance in mood, with short periods of feeling normal. "Minor depression has an off-on quality," says Dr. Stephen Hurt, a psychologist at New York Hospital in White Plains, New York. "There may be normal moods that last a few weeks, even a month." [11]

## SUBCATEGORIES OF OTHER SPECIFIC AFFECTIVE DISORDERS

### A. Dysthymic Disorder

Dysthymic disorder is similar to major depression, but the symptoms are fewer in number, less severe, and of shorter duration. To be diagnosed as having dysthymic disorder, the person must have suffered at least three of the symptoms listed below, and these symptoms must have lasted for one year in teenagers and two years in adults.

Dysthymic disorder is characterized by feeling sad, blue, down-in-the-dumps, worthless, and hopeless. These feelings seem as if they will never end, although some patients experience short periods—no more than a few days or weeks—of feeling normal. "Even if something good happens, the very depressed person feels bad," [12] says NIMH psychiatrist Jack Blaine. Dysthymic patients are often able to go on functioning, but under the heavy burden of a constant battle against depressed feelings about virtually everything.

In teenagers, social relationships are affected, as dysthymic adolescents react shyly or negatively to praise or overtures of friendship from their peers, and often respond with negative behavior to positive relationships, such as acting resentful or angry. In addition, performance in school is either negatively affected or interrupted. [13]

Dysthymic people frequently feel extremely embarrassed about how they feel, as there seems to be no obvious cause for their distress. A typical behavior is throwing away mail unread, or losing objects and not attempting to find them. These seemingly

37

irresponsible behaviors are actually caused by depressed feelings that, if they could be put into words, might be, "Nothing matters to me anymore." A twenty-year-old woman said, "At least when my life was difficult for a specific reason, I thought I had a reason to be depressed. But now, with nothing major going wrong in my life, I feel so unjustified."[14]

## B. Cyclothymic Disorder

Cyclothymic disorder is characterized by numerous periods of depression alternating with numerous periods of mild mania (hypomania). The depressed and hypomanic periods may be separated by periods of normal mood lasting for as long as several months. However, at least three symptoms listed below must have lasted for at least a year in adolescents and two years in adults.

During the depressed periods, the person loses interest or pleasure in all, or almost all, usual activities. In the hypomanic period, the person feels an elevated or irritable mood. In addition, cyclothymic disorder is characterized by an overabundance or lack of the same symptom in both states of the illness. For example, if the person feels incompetent during the depressed state, he or she will feel overly competent during the mild manic state. Other examples include sleeping too much versus decreased need for sleep; decreased attention and concentration versus sharp, alert and unusually creative thinking.

Substance abuse is particularly common in cyclothymic disorder, as people try to self-medicate themselves with alcohol or sedatives during the depressed periods, or with stimulants and psychedelic drugs during the mild manic periods.[15]

## III. ATYPICAL AFFECTIVE DISORDERS

People suffering from atypical affective disorders, which include "atypical bipolar disorder" and "atypical depression," are people suffering from mania or depression whose symptoms do not meet the criteria of any one of the above classifications.

38

## SUBCATEGORIES OF ATYPICAL AFFECTIVE DISORDERS

### A. Atypical Bipolar Disorder

This category includes people with manic symptoms that cannot be classified as bipolar disorder or as cyclothymic disorder. An example of atypical bipolar disorder is a person who previously had a major depressive episode and now has an illness with some manic features, but not of sufficient severity and duration to meet the criteria for a manic episode.

### B. Atypical Depression

This category includes people with depressive symptoms that cannot be diagnosed as a major affective or dysthymic disorder. For example, the person's symptoms meet the criteria for dysthymic disorder, but there have been periods of normal mood lasting more than a few months.[16]

"A compliment, a success, an unexpected phone call from an acquaintance can cheer them up immensely," says Dr. Quitkin. "But their good mood doesn't last long. A few hours later, they're back in the dumps."[17] Atypically depressed people reverse some of the symptoms of major depression. Instead of suffering from insomnia, they oversleep, occasionally sleeping as much as twelve to fifteen hours a day. Rather than avoiding food, they overeat; and they feel worse in the evening, rather than in the morning. Another major symptom is hypersensitivity to rejection. Trivial slights can devastate victims of atypical depression.[18]

Because these subcategories of depression tend to overlap and thus make it more difficult to diagnose the type of depression a person has, many psychiatrists use a simpler method of diagnosis in which they separate depression into two groups: endogenous and nonendogenous.

Endogenous means the illness is caused by a biological abnormality. This depression is characterized by a general lack of feeling and a sense of emptiness, rather than by a feeling of sadness. Endogenous depression, which is worse in the morning, causes distinct physical symptoms as well, including extreme lethargy (tiredness) or the opposite, severe agitation and jumpiness; and marked changes in sleeping and eating habits, such as anorexia with weight loss, and early morning insomnia. Occasionally the illness is severe enough to cause a marked distortion in the person's ability to perceive reality, and the person may have delusions and hallucinations. In addition, the person realizes he or she is experiencing a distinct change from his or her usual self and complains of loss of pleasure in almost all activities. Many psychiatrists have found antidepressant medications to be the most effective treatment, along with psychotherapy.

Nonendogenous depression is characterized by a disturbance in mood and general outlook. The physical symptoms are less severe than in endogenous depression. The person remains able to interpret reality and, "although the person never really feels like himself, he still can experience some enjoyment sometimes,"[19] says Dr. John Rush, professor and director of the Affective Disorders Unit at the University of Texas Medical School in Dallas. Nonendogenous depression often occurs in response to stressful life events that keep occurring over a long period of time and produce problems in daily living. For example, the person experiences school or job problems, sexual problems, and difficulty in personal relationships.

Often you may not think of this depression as a change from your usual self, because you have had problems in living for so long that you consider the current depressive episode simply part of your personality. You may, however, complain of a reason that caused the depression.

Soon the DSM III will include criteria for a recently discovered new subtype of depression called Seasonal Affective Disorder (SAD). SAD mainly affects people during the winter months and can be treated with special light therapy.

Almost everyone feels better during the bright days of summer than during the gray winter days when there are fewer hours of daylight. But people who suffer from SAD experience extra listlessness during fall and winter. They lose interest in joyful activities and feel sluggish, irritable, and depressed, sometimes even to the point of committing suicide. Like hibernating animals, they crave sleep. They also binge on carbohydrates.

Children and teenagers suffering from SAD complain of being tired and unhappy in school in the late fall. They increasingly sleep later as the weeks pass, have difficulty waking up, cry for no reason, and complain of physical ailments such as headaches. January and February seem to be their worst months. In a study of children six to fourteen suffering from SAD, the children were put on a light-therapy regimen, and almost all rapidly improved. A champion swimmer whose swim times always mysteriously dropped during the winter broke his previous records. A thirteen-year-old boy made the honor roll at school for his first winter ever.

The cause of SAD may be a sleep-inducing hormone called melatonin, which is produced in the dark. Some researchers believe SAD may be a biological phenomenon left over from prehistoric times when people conserved energy during the cold winter months when food was scarce. Psychiatrists are treating those afflicted with SAD with a special fluorescent light called a "SunBox," which mimics sunlight. "It's like being two different people," says one SAD sufferer. In the spring, she felt "like a bear coming out of hibernation." In the winter, she "went to work, came home and stayed inside."[20]

From 3 to 6 percent of Americans experience these milder forms of depression, according to a recent National Institute of Mental Health study. "Chronic mild depressives go to work or school, maintain relationships, but they never seem to get out from under the black cloud hanging over them," says Dr. James Kocsis, director of the Clinical Inpatient Research Unit at the Payne Whitney Clinic of New York's Cornell Medical Center. "Often they tell us they don't answer their phones because they're too down."[21]

A recent study of 120 people with atypical depression revealed that over 75 percent responded to the antidepressant drug Nardil® (phenelzine). "Within a few months . . . you see striking changes,'' says Dr. Quitkin. ''They're making friends, getting along better at work. That's amazing, since improving patients' social skills is one of the hardest things to achieve. But this happens so quickly—usually within six weeks—that we now believe these people have a flaw in their neurochemistry that kept their mood down. . . .''[22]

As one seventeen-year-old said after taking Nardil® for six weeks: ''I suddenly felt this bolt of energy. Whereas before I could barely climb the stairs to my bedroom, now I raced up them two at a time. Studying doesn't seem the drudge it used to be, and my grades have gone from Ds to Bs. Now I'm thinking about the future. Maybe a career in journalism. But what I become doesn't matter as much as the fact that I want to become.''

Teenagers often move from minor depression to major depression and back again. Deciding what type of depression a person has is tricky, due to the many factors involved—the symptoms, causes, and the individual's environment and biochemical makeup. A group of diagnostic questionnaires have been established to further help physicians accurately diagnose the type of depression a patient has.

One of the most widely used diagnostic questionnaires is the Beck Depression Inventory, developed by Dr. Aaron Beck, a professor of psychiatry at the University of Pennsylvania. In the Beck Inventory, patients choose between such contrasting statements as, ''I do not feel sad'' and ''I feel so sad I can't stand it,'' or ''I don't feel disappointed in myself'' and ''I hate myself.'' The first statement of each pair gets a zero, while the second scores high on the depression scale.

## MASKED DEPRESSION

A type of depression that shows all the symptoms of depressive illness, yet cannot be diagnosed as an actual mood disorder, is ''masked depression.'' This is depression that masquerades as madness or badness. Many teenagers who are afraid of their sad feelings or are unable to handle them cover them up by acting in an aggressive manner, such as lying, stealing, running away, abusing drugs or alcohol, driving recklessly, or becoming sexually promiscuous. Teenage girls often become pregnant, feeling that having a baby will finally give them someone who will love them.

Masked depression in teenagers can also take the form of hiding depression in physical complaints such as back pain, joint pain, stomach pain, headaches, and ulcers. Such teenagers are often thought to lack self-control or moral development. But, "in fact," says Dr. Robin Alter, clinical consultant at Toronto's Dellcrest Children's Center, "these teenagers may be all too well-developed morally, overly concerned about right and wrong. Beneath the bully or the cheat, there's fear and a sense of abandonment." [23]

As evidence of how widespread the symptoms of masked depression are, consider the following. Each year more than a million teenagers abuse alcohol, run away, or become pregnant; more than a quarter of a million teenagers attempt suicide. [24]

Dr. Mardy Wasserman, a Los Angeles clinical psychologist, says, "These behaviors may be hiding very sad, hurt or scared feelings in a teen. She doesn't know any other way of coping with the depression, but at least she feels she's getting attention. It may not be the kind of attention she'd want, but then she's not really asking for what she wants." [25]

Teenagers and children suffering from masked depression often end up being treated for hyperactivity and learning disabilities, or being punished for laziness or aggressive, destructive behavior, when they should really be treated for depression, which is the root of all their problems.

Stephen, one of Dr. Alter's patients, was a suicidal eight year old. When asked why he wanted to kill himself, he shrugged and said, "Anything is better than this." Stephen could not explain "this." His parents were conscientious and loving, yet Stephen's appearance was that of a sad, uncared-for child. His hair looked as if it hadn't been combed in months; his shoelaces were untied; and he didn't wipe his nose when it ran. "Stephen needs reassurance that he is loved and valued," Dr. Alter told his family. "You need to see his 'impossible behavior' [his masked depression] as a sign of despair and a cry for help."[26]

Psychologist David Goldstein conducted a five-year study of 159 learning-disabled children in Philadelphia and found that nearly all were depressed. In about one-third of these children, depression caused their school problems, as evidenced by the fact that when the depression lifted, their academic abilities improved dramatically.[27]

Some teenagers, like adults, may show symptoms that mimic depression, but are actually symptoms of other diseases. "When a young person can't function in his environment, refuses to go to school, or becomes very aggressive, you also have to look at whether something is going on organically," says child psychiatrist Nancy Roeske. "Every child with a problem needs a thorough physical examination. For example, at nine and ten the child is entering an age where diabetes or epilepsy may begin to show up. . . ."[28]

According to Dr. Grace Ketterman, medical director of the Crittenton Center in Kansas City, Missouri, there are five major types of masked depression in teenagers:

1. *Fatigue due to rapid physical development.* As teenagers physically develop into adults, an enormous amount of physical energy is burned up. At times, this makes nearly all adolescents feel as if they have no energy.
2. *Disturbed family relationships.* When teenagers cannot resolve arguments or problems with their parents, they may show symptoms of depression, such as staying in their rooms, sulking, spending more time away from home, or talking to their parents in an angry, disrespectful manner.
3. *Temporary moodiness—the blues.* All teenagers occasionally suffer from "the blues." The cause often stems from the typical self-scrutiny teenagers engage in. They find fault with their hair, eyes, skin, bodies, intelligence, clothes, and talents. Teenagers also get depressed if someone else finds fault with them, such as being laughed at for not knowing an an-

swer to a question in class, not being invited to a party, failing a test, or not having a date for the prom. They interpret such incidents to mean rejection of or worthlessness in themselves. But in teenagers not suffering from a major depressive illness, these moods of despair last only from a few hours to a few days and are interwoven with happy plans for the future.

4. *Minigrief episodes.* One of the most common look-alikes of depression is grief. In fact, unresolved grief forms the basis for most real depression. For a teenager, grief can come from moving to another city, the death of a relative, or the divorce of parents. For these losses, comfort and reassurance from parents and friends, along with time, are all that is needed to heal the grief. In true depression, however, the teenager can rarely remember the event that caused the sadness. Professional help is needed to uncover the original cause of the depression.

5. *Chemical addiction.* Drug and alcohol abuse is the major mimicker of depression among young people. Yet most drug and alcohol abuse is actually the result of underlying depression. With all the stresses of being a teenager, a way to feel good quickly—by taking a pill, a smoke, or a drink—becomes an irresistible solution to feeling sad. Dependency on these chemicals then often results, and teenagers get caught in a web of crimes and drug-dealing to pay for their habit. Thus there is grief due to loss even in drug dependency, as these teenagers have lost the freedom to live their lives without the help of drugs.[29]

Another mimicker of depression common among adolescents is decreased functioning of the thyroid gland, which shows up in depressive symptoms such as fatigue, difficulty in concentrating, and increased sleeping.

Women often become depressed due to changes in the levels of hormones in their bodies. One of the most common examples of this type of masked depression is "Premenstrual Syndrome" (PMS). Each month, from a few days to as long as two weeks before a woman starts her menstrual period, changes in her hormone levels may cause her to feel short-tempered, moody, sad, or hopeless. After starting her period, the depression vanishes, and the woman feels like her old self again.

Other women get depressed while taking birth control pills. And still other women suffer depression for about a month after childbirth. This is called "Postpartum Depression."

While it may seem that diagnosing the type of depression a person has cannot be exact, and therefore not important, classifying depressed patients is vital in order to determine proper treatment. For without proper treatment, any hope of relieving the depression and being able to lead a normal life is greatly reduced, if not impossible to attain.

# 4
# MANIC-DEPRESSIVE ILLNESS

*"Melancholy is the curse of frenzy."*

*—William Shakespeare*

Shakespeare could not have been more on target when describing manic-depressive (bipolar) illness. An estimated four million Americans suffer from the disease. In manic-depressive illness, a person switches from a depressed mood, with all the symptoms of severe depression, to a euphoric (elated) mood, characterized by feeling either on top of the world or extremely irritable.[1]

A manic or depressive attack may strike without any known cause, or be triggered by a stressful event such as a personal loss. The attacks may last from weeks to months to years, depending upon whether or not the person gets proper treatment. The depressive stage tends to develop slowly over a period of days, weeks, or months, while the manic stage is more likely to appear abruptly. Both stages may disappear abruptly as well, without any known reason.[2]

In the intervals between attacks, the person's mood, thinking, and behavior return to normal. This "well time" usually lasts several months, but some patients are "rapid cyclers"—they go through four or more mood swings in a few months. At the other extreme, some patients go through a mood swing only every five years or so.

Along with the dramatic ups and downs in mood are changes in activity—from slow and tired movements in the depressed stage to hyperactivity in the manic stage, as if the person is acting in a fast-speed film, in which everything in their lives accelerates, including thinking, conversation, and activities.[3]

The disease affects both males and females, all personality types, and all ethnic and racial groups about equally. The first attack usually occurs when the person is in the teens or early twenties. However, cases have occurred in very young children. The average number of attacks in a lifetime is thirteen. In some instances, mania and depression occur so far apart in patients that they will be admitted into a hospital for severe depression, discharged when they are better, and then months, or even years, later, the same individual will be admitted into the hospital suffering from mania.[4]

## CAUSES OF MANIC-DEPRESSION

Thought to be the most biologically caused form of all types of depressive illness, manic-depression is a result of chemical imbalances in the brain, many scientists believe. Researchers are especially studying norepinephrine, a chemical released in the brain that regulates mood. Many scientists believe that some depressions may be linked to a lack of norepinephrine, whereas some manias may be linked to an excess of this chemical.

A second theory developed by Dr. Frederick K. Goodwin and Dr. Thomas A. Wehr of NIMH proposes that manic-depressive illness is linked to a disturbance of the body's "biological clock" that synchronizes the body's daily activities with external events such as day and night. In manic-depressive patients, they found that the timing of three crucial body rhythms—sleep, body temperature, and release of certain hormones—is abnormal, with the highs and lows of energy occurring several hours earlier than usual. According to Dr. Wehr, "This finding could indicate that the biological clock in these patients is speeded up, like a watch that runs fast."[5]

Bipolar depression is also believed to have a genetic basis, as the illness seems to occur more in families whose members have some form of depression. Although researchers have been unable to find a single gene that transmits vulnerability to manic-depressive illness, in a study conducted by scientists at the University of Miami School of Medicine, researchers studied an eighty-one-member Amish family in Pennsylvania. After talking to them and sampling their blood for genetic material, nearly 80 percent of this family's members were found to have had manic depression, and those members were found to have a genetic marker—an identifiable pattern of genetic material—on one of their chromosomes. These scientists believe that people who inherit this genetic marker also inherit a gene along with it that makes them liable to get manic-depressive illness.[6]

In another study, 27 percent of children with one manic-depressive parent developed the disorder themselves; when both parents suffered manic-depressive illness, 74 percent of their children did as well. When manic-depressive illness occurs in adolescence, there is nearly always a strong family history of depression.[7]

## SYMPTOMS OF
## MANIC-DEPRESSIVE ILLNESS

Bipolar depression is one of the most frustrating diseases to experience, and one of the most sorrowful for anyone who cares about the person suffering from the illness to watch, as people in a manic state do not know their behavior appears odd or "crazy" to others.

General symptoms of mania include twitching of the eyes and lips, funny tastes in the mouth, an inability to bear hearing loud noises, overtalkativeness, distractibility, grandiosity, delusions, financial extravagance, sleep problems, "flight of ideas"—a

49

continuous, fast speech with abrupt changes from topic to topic—and racing thoughts. Manic patients complain their thoughts run so fast that their ability to verbalize their ideas can't keep up.

A specific symptom of mania includes being in continual motion while talking loudly, constantly, and rapidly, usually with an overflow of ideas are related to each other, but hard to follow because of the person's rapid speech. Sometimes the manic person will skip from one subject to another, only to come back to the original subject several hours later. Some manic people make jokes and puns, becoming the life of the party. Others become so sarcastic and irritable, they drive friends away.

If you listen to someone talk while he's in a manic stage, you will hear fleeting periods of depression within their elated chatter. A seventeen-year-old boy was talking about feeling on top of the world and his plans for the future, when suddenly he started talking about feeling guilty over an incident that happened when he was ten. One day he had become so angry at his younger brother that he pushed him off his bicycle, resulting in a broken ankle for the younger boy. In the middle of his story, the boy's depressed expression switched to a smile, and he started chattering away about his plans for the prom, as if his sudden guilty memory had never occurred.

An offshoot of this rush of talking and flight of ideas is an urge to be overly sociable, such as making long distance phone calls to friends at any time of the day or night, and talking for hours. It is not uncommon for manic people to telephone strangers all over the world, racking up huge phone bills.

Because their mood can be disorganized, flamboyant, and bizarre, they often wear clashing, bright, mismatched, or strange clothes. Or they may dye their hair an odd color and cut it in an offbeat style. Girls typically wear excessive, poorly applied makeup. Feeling overly generous, they give away money, food, or advice to strangers they pass on the street.

Manic people involve themselves in every activity they can find, and become extremely irritable or angry if anyone tries to stop them from pursuing these activities. Because they overextend themselves, they become extremely frustrated when they cannot accomplish every feat or project they start or when their attempts turn out a shambles.

For example, a high school student may be the editor of the school paper, a cheerleader, a volunteer in a day-care center, the head of the prom committee, a girl scout, and the soloist in the church choir. In every activity, she tries to take on the role of chief organizer, in effect trying to do in very little time what would take even the most industrious person a lot longer to accomplish.

Another typical symptom of this illness is spending a great amount of money on unnecessary things. In adults, this habit often takes the form of charging to the limit on credit cards, whether or not they have the money in their bank accounts to pay the bills; buying and selling cars one after the other; or speculating in the stock market.

When mania shows itself as irritability, arguing, or sarcasm, the manic person is unbearable to be around. He or she interferes with the lives of friends and family, irritating them to the point where they withdraw from the manic person. Manic people express opinions on *any* subject. For example, a sixteen-year-old criticizes her mother's clothes as being either too old-looking or too young-looking, then goes on for as long as the mother will listen about how her mother's earrings are a slight shade too blue for the dress she's wearing. If the mother does not interrupt, her daughter could talk nonstop all night about the different shades of blue and what shade goes with what.

Or a teenage boy might complain that his room is too small, then go on to complain about every little detail about his house that needs repairing or is not perfect to him. He will nag his parents about what is wrong with the house for as long as they are willing to listen. In other words, the manic person makes an encyclopedic amount of comments on what is actually worth about one sentence.

Another feature of the manic stage is inflated self-esteem, called grandiosity, in which the person feels he or she is all-powerful and can do anything. Manic grandiosity is different from the feelings of immortality and the "I can get away with anything"

51

belief that many teenagers experience during adolescent development, such as they can get away with disobeying traffic rules, lying to parents, cheating on exams, or abusing drugs or alcohol without hurting their bodies.

An example of grandiosity in manic-depressive illness is teenagers who, despite an obvious lack of talent in a particular activity, believe they are extremely talented in that activity and should be recognized for their talent. A teenager might believe he is a talented guitar player, although he has never had a lesson. He will attempt to play the guitar, fully believing he is playing the hottest rock music anyone has ever heard. In reality, the music is merely loud noise.

Another form of grandiosity is thinking up extravagant ideas, combined with a know-it-all attitude, but exhibiting no judgment. For an adult, this may involve investing in an unsound business venture, such as building a summer resort on a barren island in the cold North Sea. The person is sure the resort will make a fortune, even though he or she has not bothered to check out any of the details, including the cost, of putting the idea into action.

Grandiosity may also take the form of giving advice on subjects about which the person has no knowledge, such as how to run the United Nations. A teenage boy may get into a long discussion with the school principal about how the school should be run more efficiently. He might even go so far as to write countless letters, make daily phone calls, or pay weekly visits to the board of education, insisting they incorporate his ideas.

Because manic-depressive people are overstimulated, they need little or no sleep, and they often stay up for days at a time without feeling tired. When they do lie down, their minds race so rapidly they are unable to fall asleep. A teenager who plays in a neighborhood band might stay up all night writing what she believes to be the greatest song to hit the charts since the Beatles, only to come down from the manic stage and realize she has written nothing but gibberish. By the same token, other manic people imagine themselves to be great writers and stay awake for days writing what they believe will be the next *Gone with the Wind,* only to discover when their mania lifts that nothing they have written makes any sense.

Other manic-depressives become overstimulated sexually and engage in promiscuous sexual behavior. Since the advent of AIDS, this symptom has taken on life-threatening overtones.

Besides the possibility of acting violently if their wishes are not fulfilled, another frightening feature of the disease is the seemingly "crazy" or bizarre behavior the individuals often exhibit. This behavior seems to go with their grandiose, "I'm smarter than anyone" frame of mind. A common bizarre habit is chuckling or talking to themselves.

One teenager went up and down the aisles of a video store chuckling at the other customers and muttering criticisms about how the store was run. When his sister asked what was so funny, he became extremely angry, shouting, "You're too stupid to understand." By the time they left the store, the sister was in tears, as the other kids were looking at her brother as if he were insane. Later, when her brother came out of the manic stage, he had no memory of his behavior in the video store.

Delusions and hallucinations are also seen in mania. Grandiose delusions are often of a religious nature, such as the person believing he or she has a special relationship with God and has been chosen by God for a special purpose in life. Other times manic people believe they are good friends with a well-known celebrity or political figure, or are descended from royalty, such as being related to the Queen of England. Occasionally manic delusions take the form of irrational fears, such as the fear that one is being controlled by an outside force or person.

These delusions and hallucinations may make people in a manic state seem to be suffering from schizophrenia, a disease characterized by bizarre thoughts or obsessions. One teenage girl believed her thoughts and words were being collected by radio, then transmitted by television throughout the state.[8] But in contrast to schizophrenia, manic delusions usually start abruptly, vary in content in the same person, and do not last long.

Some scientists believe there are three states of manic-depressive illness. The early stage, called hypomania, seems to promote creativity and accomplishment. During hypomania, the person feels as though on a mild high. Fueled by limitless energy, hypomanics can function on just a few hours' sleep a night. Brilliant thoughts flash into their minds, and they become extremely productive at whatever they do, such as studying for a test, writing, or painting.[9]

Many great artists, writers, musicians, actors, and political leaders have suffered from the illness. Frederick Goodwin, a scientific director of NIMH, says that 38 percent of all Pulitzer Prize-winning poets have had the criteria of manic-depressive illness. Composers such as Berlioz, Mahler, and Handel, author Virginia Woolf, former President Teddy Roosevelt, and actresses Kristy McNichols and Patty Duke, have also had bipolar depression. Before the discovery of lithium, many manic-depressives actually died of exhaustion.[10]

Dr. Michael J. Gitlin, director of the Affective Disorders Clinic at UCLA Medical Center in Los Angeles, says, "If you get too manic, things get fragmented and disorganized. Hypomania is a very creative state of being; the problem is you can't control it."[11]

Yet in spite of the many masterpieces these artists produced during their manic highs, they also had to endure the havoc of the second and third stages of manic-depressive illness as well. During the second stage, a full-blown manic attack occurs, with symptoms ranging from irritability, grandiosity, bragging about talents and physical attributes, paranoia, agitation, explosions of aggressiveness when crossed, alcoholism, and lack of good judgment.

In the third stage, feelings of elation are replaced by feelings of being disorganized and out of control. Manic people become frightened, confused, lost in the twisting mazes of their own minds. Their talk is impossible to follow, and their symptoms often cannot be distinguished from the excited type of schizophrenia.

Hallucinations are common here, with many patients believing they have miraculous powers, such as psychic abilities enabling them to predict the future. Typical behavior is phoning religious leaders and even the White House to rant about their powers. In some cases, patients become psychotic (out of touch with reality), requiring hospitalization. Psychotic symptoms are particularly common among manic-depressives who become ill in their teens and twenties. In about one-third of these teenage cases, delusions and hallucinations take over the more common manic symptoms of hyperactivity.[12]

According to Dr. Paula J. Clayton, chairman of psychiatry at the University of Minnesota Medical School, "a psychotic episode in adolescence is more likely to be caused by manic-depressive illness than by any other disorder. Manic-depressive teenagers often are mislabeled schizophrenic or emotionally disturbed—an error that results in disastrously inappropriate therapy, as they may be denied lithium, for instance. Adolescent mania is particularly crippling. These young patients lose their chance for a normal adolescence in terms of establishing relationships with their peers."[13] Manic-depressive illness is different from schizophrenia, however, in that, unlike schizophrenics, most manic-depressives do not deteriorate mentally.

In a milder form of manic-depressive illness, called cyclothymia, the manic and depressive episodes are shorter, less intense, and switch rapidly, each lasting only a few days. Other people think of cyclothymic people as moody. They are usually able to function without psychiatric help. The possibility does exist, however, that a cyclothymic person will at some point develop severe attacks of mania or depression.

Jennifer, a cyclothymic high school senior, was thought by her teachers to be a bright underachiever because of her alternating strong and weak academic motivation. On "bad" days, Jennifer was oversensitive, insecure, and tired. Any confrontation made her cry. On "good" days, which could last up to a week, she became a conscientious, able student. She was also, however, argumentative with both her teachers and friends, and often failed to finish projects.

Such self-defeating behavior is typical of cyclothymic people. In a college student, such behavior is often seen by their constantly switching majors. According to Dr. Clayton, cyclothymic people often fail to reach their full potential as adults. Their career goals depend upon their mood at the moment. The medication lithium controls these mood swings. Cyclothymic patients on lithium still feel some ups and downs, but not so severe that they burst into tears at the slightest provocation. Nor do they become so hyperactive that they are irritated with the rest of the world for moving so slowly.

## TREATMENT FOR
## MANIC-DEPRESSIVE ILLNESS

Manic-depressive illness is one of the easiest types of depression to treat. The major medication used to help restore chemical imbalances in the brain, and thus lessen or eliminate the cycles of depression and mania, is lithium. This antidepressant usually stops all symptoms of mania within one to three weeks, sometimes even within hours of taking the drug. In some cases, the attacks become less frequent, shorter, milder, and less likely to require hospitalization, although lithium does not eliminate the attacks entirely.

Lithium is a naturally occurring substance that is in the same chemical group as sodium and potassium. In ancient Rome, physicians sent their manic patients to certain springs now known to contain high levels of lithium in its mineral form. Today several million patients around the world take the drug on a regular basis. Most experts believe that any person who has had at least two manic attacks should be considered for lithium use, provided the drug is effective and does not cause major side effects.[14]

The discovery that lithium can be used to treat manic-depressive illness occurred relatively by accident. In 1949, a psychiatrist who was giving lithium to guinea pigs noticed that the drug produced a sedative effect in the pigs. This gave him the idea that it might be used to treat mania.

In the late 1940s, lithium was used as a salt substitute in the United States. Many people who used too much "salt" at one time died from lithium poisoning. If the body contains too much of the chemical, it produces bad side effects, such as diarrhea, weight loss, tremors, slurred speech, dizziness, convulsions, confusion, restlessness, stupor, coma, heart, thyroid, and kidney problems, and even circulatory collapse. No pregnant woman should ever take lithium, as it can cause damage to the fetus. Less severe side effects are excessive thirst and weight gain.

The answer to using lithium safely is to keep the level of lithium in the blood from rising too high or too quickly. This is done by taking frequent blood tests, and then increasing or decreasing the dosage according to how much or how little lithium is in the blood. When the medication is first begun, a blood test should be taken within one or two days.

Because everyone's body chemistry is different, a safe blood level for one person may not be safe for another. That is why people taking lithium must be under the care of a physician who monitors their blood levels. After the lithium dosage is regulated, the patient has a blood test once each week for about a month, then once a month, then, if the patient's lithium blood level appears to have stabilized, once every three months, or as often as the doctor recommends.[15]

Today lithium is recognized to be as effective in treating manic-depressive illness as antibiotics are in treating infectious diseases. No other drug in psychiatry has been studied as much. One interesting result of the research is that lithium has been proven strongest in terms of prevention. This means that a person who has been diagnosed as manic-depressive, but who is not currently experiencing a manic episode, can take lithium to prevent an attack of mania. Lithium has also been shown effective in treating people with depression only.

Cheryl, now nineteen, has suffered from manic-depressive illness since she was ten.

> Each time I'd get depressed, I'd kind of slide into it. First I'd get real grouchy. Then I'd get lazy and not want to do anything. I'd skip school, quit caring about going to the movies or to the mall. Eventually I

57

wouldn't even go outside. I'd get so low that just moving my jaw took more energy than I could handle, so I didn't talk.

Then one day I woke up feeling high, like I could do anything. I tried, too. I joined all the clubs at school, got the lead in the senior play, and started playing tennis in city competitions. Then I would have this weird urge to buy things. I'd steal money or credit cards out of my mom's purse and go on a shopping binge. I didn't need even a fourth of the things I bought. Like five pairs of the same jeans, or ten T-shirts all the same color blue. I couldn't sleep at night, so I'd phone my friends at all hours. Boy, did I get laid into by their folks. Once I even telephoned Paris, France. I thought my dad would croak when he got that phone bill.

I lost my best friend because of those highs. One day I was driving us to the mall, and suddenly this feeling like I was Wonder Woman came over me. I started going about 80 miles per hour down this curving road, skipping stop signs and running red lights. I thought I could survive anything. It seems crazy now, but that day I believed I was like Wily Coyote in those "Road Runner" cartoons, where old Wily crashes his jalopy into a building and comes out on the other side with just a few scratches. So instead of parking in the lot, I drove straight through the front door of the mall. But unlike Wily Coyote, my friend and I came out with more than a few scratches. We ended up staying in the hospital for a month with broken bones and concussions.

Because my folks thought I was trying to kill myself by driving into a building, they sent a psychiatrist to see me while I was in the hospital. After about a week of talking to her, she said she thought all the ups and downs I was going through were caused by an illness. That was the first time I had ever heard

58

the word "manic-depression." She asked if I'd try this medicine. By then I was so sick of my roller coaster moods, I would have tried arsenic.

The medicine was lithium, and it stopped what I called "my crazies." I started going to group therapy with other kids who had manic-depressive illness. I felt better knowing I wasn't the only one who had it. A bunch of those kids had actually done the same nutty things I had. But some stopped taking lithium after awhile. They said they felt fine and weren't going to mess up their heads with drugs. Some drug. Ha! In about two days they were just as manic as ever. Taking lithium isn't any different than taking insulin if you're diabetic. So if you have manic-depression, don't quit lithium until your doctor says to. Trust me. That drug will change your life.

Lithium has changed the lives of countless people like Cheryl. People have gone from a miserable, embarrassing, and potentially dangerous existence for themselves and those around them, to a life filled with hope, dignity, and peace of mind.

Unfortunately, 25 percent of all manic-depressive people, most of whom have four or more episodes a year, show no response to lithium. For these patients, a new drug called carbamazepine is currently under investigation. The results so far seem promising.

# 5
# ANTIDEPRESSANT MEDICATIONS

In 1956, a medication used to treat tuberculosis was found to have uplifting side effects. Doctors thought perhaps the medication could be given to depressed patients to help their sad moods.

Scientists tried to find what chemicals produced by the brain affect a person's mood, and how much or how little of those chemicals lift a person's mood out of depression. They discovered that the two most important neurochemicals that normalize a person's feelings of well-being are serotonin and norepinephrine. Researchers experimented on developing drugs that would regulate the amount of these chemicals released by the brain. They succeeded, and in 1958 the first tricyclic antidepressant medication, ''imipramine,'' was produced.[1]

Tricyclics, named because of their three-ring structure, work by causing the brain to produce more serotonin and norepinephrine. On the other hand, antidepressants that help manic-depressive people work by decreasing the amounts of brain chemicals produced, thus lowering their elevated moods to a normal level.[2]

Recently, tetracyclic antidepressants (with four cyclic or ring structures) have become available, such as maprotiline (brand name Ludiomil®), and trazodone (brand name Desyrel®), which seem to cause fewer side effects.[3]

Accurate diagnosis of whether a person has a depressive illness, and if so, which type, is critical to avoid being given the wrong medication and suffering serious side effects, as well as a worsening of the depression.

The doctor who is most qualified to accurately diagnose depressive illness and prescribe the correct medication, if needed, is a psychiatrist. Psychiatrists are medical doctors, whereas psychologists and social workers are not. And only medical doctors can prescribe medication.

In addition, most nonpsychiatric physicians, such as internists and family practitioners, have not studied psychological medications and their effects on a person's mood. Therefore, they are not as familiar with which antidepressants are available and which work best for what types of depression. Most psychiatrists on the other hand, have had training in psychopharmacology, the study of psychological medications. This knowledge is necessary to distinguish between less severe psychological depression (which may require psychotherapy only to relieve the depression) and chemical depression (which usually requires an antidepressant to relieve symptoms, as well as psychotherapy).[4]

Seeing a psychiatrist does not mean you are mentally ill. Thousands of people go to psychiatrists for problems ranging in severity from deep depression to difficulty in making friends, dating, shyness, lack of self-esteem, or getting along with parents. In order to decide if an antidepressant medication will help your depression, or whether some form of psychotherapy alone will help, the psychiatrist will ask you about which symptoms of depression you have been experiencing, such as weight loss, crying spells, or restlessness.

The psychiatrist will also want to know what is going on in your life, including any problems you experienced before you felt depressed, or are now experiencing, and if you have had any previous treatment for depression. If so, the psychiatrist will ask what the effects of the treatment were. Because depressive illnesses often run in families, the psychiatrist will also want to know whether any other members of your family have ever been diagnosed as depressed. A relative's illness may provide an important clue to the psychiatrist in diagnosing your type of depression.

An effective treatment for one type of depression may be ineffective or even harmful for another kind of depression. Many physicians believe medication relieves the depressive symptoms, while psychotherapy helps people change their way of thinking and relating to others in order to improve their self-image and relationships. Seriously depressed people are often too sad and tired, and unable to think clearly enough to deal with their life problems with the help of psychotherapy alone until an antidepressant lifts their mood to a more normal level.[5]

Over 80 percent of biological depressions respond to one of the antidepressant drugs. Sometimes a psychiatrist will prescribe two different antidepressants to be taken by the same patient. Depression that has reached the psychotic stage, in which the person has delusions or hallucinations and has lost touch with reality, usually requires an antidepressant medication plus an antipsychotic drug, such as chlorpromazine (Thorazine®), haloperidol (Haldol®) or thiothixene (Navene®).[6]

If you do take an antidepressant medication, it is necessary that a physician monitor the medication. This means that you see your doctor on a regular basis to make sure you are taking the correct dosage and that you are not experiencing any serious side effects.

How you feel is one of the best ways to determine whether an antidepressant is helping, and if not, whether the dosage needs to be increased or decreased. Sleeping better is often one of the first improvements, followed by renewed appetite, and eventually by a feeling of hope and renewed energy.[7]

Another way to determine the correct dosage is by being given a blood test that shows your doctor how much medication is in your blood. Dosages often need to be increased or decreased, depending upon the medication level in the blood. Everyone's body chemistry is different. Thus, everyone absorbs and excretes these drugs differently. There is not one prescribed drug or dosage for everyone.

The most common reason for an antidepressant not to work is too low a dosage. In addition to blood tests, monitoring your antidepressant medication involves your doctor regularly taking your blood pressure, pulse, and an electrocardiograph (EKG) to check your heart.[8]

There are several types of antidepressants. It is an unfortunate but true fact that finding the right antidepressant medication is often a matter of trial and error. If the first medication does not help you feel less depressed after about six weeks, or if side effects become so severe that an adequate dose of a particular drug cannot be given, then your doctor will prescribe another antidepressant. Most side effects, however, usually decrease after a person's body has grown accustomed to the medication.[9]

The risk of severe side affects with an antidepressant drug used in the correct amount is, in most cases, much lower than the risk of taking penicillin or having a general anesthesia. Common side effects of antidepressants are dry mouth, constipation, light-headedness when standing, increased appetite, weight gain, drowsiness, blurred vision, difficulty urinating, and an increased heart rate. Infrequent side effects include skin rash, restlessness, sweating, agitation, mild shaking, and decreased sleep.[10]

Many people hesitate to take antidepressants, based upon misconceptions about the drugs' effects. Some people think antidepressants make a person high, like cocaine and marijuana. The truth is antidepressants do *not* produce a high or a "kick." Rather, they normalize a depressed person's mood. In fact, if taken by nondepressed people, they may produce a slight slowing down in mental capability.

Further, drugs that do make people "high," such as amphetamines, are stimulants that increase a person's energy regardless of what that person's energy level was when he or she took the amphetamine. Antidepressants, on the other hand, do not automatically increase energy or lighten mood. Instead, antidepressants increase or decrease a person's energy or mood based upon what the level of energy or mood was at the time the person took the antidepressant.

Another myth is that, like illegal drugs, antidepressant drugs can be abused. Antidepressant drugs do not create abusive use because they do not produce elated feelings. Therefore, there is no reason for a nondepressed person to want to take an antidepressant to get high. As proof of their nonabusive nature, consider that antidepressants have been in use for more than thirty years and have never been sold on the street.

Still another misconception is that antidepressants are addictive. In contrast to illegal drugs, depressed patients can stop taking any of these medications without bringing about either withdrawal symptoms or a craving for the medication. Patients who need to continue antidepressants do so because their depression will recur if they stop the medication, not because the medication has produced chemical dependency. A depressed person who continues to need an antidepressant is dependent on the medication the same way a person with diabetes is dependent on insulin—to control the symptoms of an illness. When the symptoms disappear, the medication can be stopped.

And unlike abusable drugs, in which people develop a tolerance for the drug and therefore must increase the amount taken in order to get the same feeling, once the correct dosage of an antidepressant is established that person continues feeling well while on that dosage. He or she does not have to increase the dosage to get the same effects. Any increase in dosage is based upon the results of a blood test showing there is not enough of the medication in the blood, and therefore certain symptoms are recurring.

In addition, whereas tranquilizers and stimulants produce effects within an hour, the effects of antidepressant drugs rarely begin until two to four weeks after the first dosage, and often require six weeks to reach their maximum effectiveness. Another reason why a particular antidepressant may not work is that it is not given for a long enough time. Further, all the benefits do not occur together. Insomnia may disappear in a week and appetite may return in two weeks.

Antidepressants do not affect the illness itself, but rather control the symptoms while the person's depression is running its course. In this way, antidepressants are similar to aspirin, which controls the fever of flu, but does not shorten the duration of the flu. If antidepressants are stopped too soon, the person may relapse into depression. That is why most psychiatrists wait six months after the medication starts working before they consider gradually reducing the dose down to no medication. If symptoms do not reappear when the dosage is reduced, the depressive episode has probably run its course, and the medication can be discontinued.[11]

There are three general types of antidepressants: tricyclics, monoamine oxidase inhibitors (MAOs), and lithium carbonate.

## TRICYCLIC ANTIDEPRESSANTS

*Imipramine* (Tofranil, Janimine, Sk-Pramine)
*Amitriptyline* (Elavil, Endep, Amitid)
*Amoxapine* (Ascendin)
*Desipramine* (Norpramin, Pertofrane)
*Doxepin* (Adapin, Sinequan)
*Fluoxetine* (Prozac)
*Nortriptyline* (Aventyl, Pamelor)
*Protriptyline* (Vivactil)
*Trimipramine* (Surmontil)
*Alprazolam* (Xanax) (used as an antidepressant for those
    who suffer from depression combined with anxiety)

There is little difference in effectiveness among tricyclics. Which one is prescribed first is up to the individual's doctor. If a person does not respond to the first medication, then another tricyclic may be tried. Differences in side effects may determine the use of one medication over another in different people. Most tricyclics may be taken in a single dose at bedtime so that many side effects occur when the person is asleep. For some people, however, divided doses work best.

To be effective, tricyclics must be taken regularly until depression lifts, and then they are usually continued for three months to a year after to prevent a recurrence of depression. Recent studies have shown that continued use of tricyclic antidepressants prevents recurrence of depression in patients whose depression has lifted.[12]

## MONOAMINE OXIDASE INHIBITOR
## ANTIDEPRESSANTS (MAOS)

MAO inhibitors relieve depression by inhibiting, or preventing, the enzyme monoamine oxidase from breaking down serotonin and norepinephrine, so they cannot work as neurotransmitters in the brain.[13]

Currently there are three MAO antidepressants available: isocarboxazid (Marplan®), tranylcypromine (Parnate®), and phenelzine (Nardil®). According to studies at the New York State Psychiatric Institute, Nardil® is the most effective drug yet tested for atypical depression.

MAO inhibitors are usually taken in divided doses. Their side effects are similar to those in tricyclics, with an important addition: The interaction between MAO inhibitors and certain foods and drugs containing tyramine (a neurotransmitter that affects blood pressure) causes high blood pressure. If untreated, high blood pressure breaks blood vessels in the brain and causes heart attacks and strokes.[14] Symptoms of high blood pressure are severe headaches, stiff neck, palpitating heart beat, and, less frequently, nausea, vomiting, and dilated pupils.

Foods to avoid while on an MAO inhibitor include aged cheeses; yogurt; concentrated yeast or meat extracts used in stews and certain drinks (baked products using yeast are allowed); pickled herring; liver; alcohol, wine, and beer; broad bean pods (limas, fava, Chinese, English, and so forth); canned figs; pickled, fermented, smoked, or aged meat, fish, or poultry; caffeine in large amounts; and chocolate in large amounts.

In addition, there are medications that, when combined with an MAO inhibitor, can cause high blood pressure or other severe reactions. Such medicines include *all* illegal street drugs; barbiturates; some oral diabetic medicines; "Levodopa,®" a drug used to treat Parkinson's disease; over-the-counter cold, cough, and nasal decongestant medications; Demerol®, a pain drug; amphetamines, such as diet pills; and any medication containing "epinephrine," a blood-pressure-raising hormone commonly found in anesthetics and certain novocaines. *Epinephrine and amphetamines can be fatal if combined with an MAO inhibitor.*[15]

Be sure to tell your dentist you cannot take novocaine containing epinephrine. There is another kind of novocaine that can be substituted that has no epinephrine. It is a good idea to keep a card in your purse or wallet stating you are on an MAO inhibitor, and that you cannot take any medicine containing epinephrine. Thus, if you become unconscious in an accident, for instance, the physician or hospital staff will be aware of this fact.

If you are going to have surgery, tell your surgeon you are on antidepressants, whether tricyclics, MAO inhibitors, or lithium, as most physicians will ask you to stop taking the antidepressant for a period of time before surgery. Because of such dietary and medication restrictions, psychiatrists usually prescribe tricyclics before MAO inhibitors.

## LITHIUM

Lithium (discussed in Chapter Four) is most commonly used to treat manic-depressive illness. However, lithium is occasionally used to treat people who have only depression, without any of the manic symptoms. Researchers at NIMH have found that 60 percent of manic-depressives who do not respond to lithium do well on carbamazepine (Tegretol®), an anticonvulsant drug for epileptics. The disadvantage is that Tegretol® may impair bone-marrow function and cause blood abnormalities. Combinations of any of the three types of antidepressants are sometimes effective when single drugs fail to help a person's depression.

## WAYS TO DEAL WITH
## COMMON SIDE EFFECTS

There are several ways to help relieve the common side effects of antidepressants. For dry mouth, try sips of water, sugarless hard candy and gum, and saliva-stimulating gum such as Quench.® In some cases, physicians prescribe a saliva-stimulating medication (pilocarpine).

Constipation can be lessened by eating fruits, vegetables, and sources of bulk such as bran, as well as by drinking plenty of liquids. Regular meals, sleep, and exercise also help. If the constipation does not respond to diet, a physician might prescribe a stool softener such as Retutol®, or a bulk laxative such as Metamucil®.

Lightheadedness or dizziness is usually due to a temporary drop in blood pressure that can be either caused or aggravated by antidepressants. Normally, dizziness may be prevented by standing up slowly, or when getting out of bed, first sitting up for several seconds before standing. Drinking adequate liquids prevents becoming dehydrated, which can worsen dizziness.

Sleepiness may lessen as your body grows accustomed to the medication. Your doctor may suggest taking most or all of your medication prior to bedtime, so most of the sedative effects will occur while you are asleep. During the first months of using an antidepressant, you should be especially careful while driving.

When switching from one tricyclic to another, some doctors prefer that you have a "time off" period before beginning the next antidepressant. Other doctors decrease the dosage of the first drug while increasing the dosage of the second until you are only taking the second antidepressant.

When switching from a tricyclic to an MAO inhibitor, you will probably need to discontinue the tricyclic for two weeks before starting the MAO. Lithium, however, may be added to either a tricyclic or an MAO inhibitor, so you will not have to go for long without medication if switching to lithium.[16]

Dr. Frederick Goodwin, a scientific director of NIMH, gives a chilling picture of patients' lives before antidepressant drugs: "Not counting the suicides, unipolar depressives could expect to spend about a quarter of their adult lives in hospitals, and manic-depressives about half."[17] That is why, in spite of antidepressants' side effects, in surveys of depressed people, the overwhelming majority said they would not trade their medication and resulting dry mouth, constipation, or dizziness, for the debilitating symptoms of depression.

"In the future," says Dr. Steven Paul, chief of clinical neuroscience at NIMH, "we'll look back at the way we treat depression now, and it will seem like the way doctors treated fever in the old days—by applying wet sheets."[18]

# 6
# PSYCHOTHERAPY AND
# OTHER THERAPIES

Sixteen-year-old Kim lay on her bed staring at the ceiling. A pair of earphones encircled her head, the ends attached to a cassette player. Bruce Springsteen was blaring out her favorite song, but Kim hardly heard a word. Thoughts of Heather's sweet sixteen birthday party tonight swirled through her mind. Should she go? Kim hadn't been to a party in over a year, not since she'd developed a deep depression that had gotten worse and worse until even her friends didn't want to be around her. Who wanted to hang out with someone who felt bummed all the time? Her boyfriend had broken up with her, saying he couldn't stand her moping around like she expected a nuclear bomb to hit any minute.

That was when Kim quit looking at herself in the mirror. She hated seeing that ugly, fat, dumb, clumsy girl staring back at her. Where had the petite, smart girl with the pretty red hair and sparkly green eyes gone? Kim skipped meals, lost ten pounds in a month, refused to leave her room except for school, and

70

quit talking on the phone to her friends or having them over. All she felt like doing was curling up in bed and crying.

At first her parents thought she was just going through the normal teenage ups and downs. They told her to "buckle up." She'd outgrow feeling sad. It was just a stage. But Kim didn't outgrow her "teenage blues." The hurt inside her squeezed out all the good feelings Kim had left. She quit eating altogether and lost the strength to do anything but sleep.

At the urging of the family doctor, Kim was admitted to the adolescent psychiatric unit of the university hospital. What Kim had was not just normal teenage blues. She was suffering from major depression. While in the hospital, she was put on the antidepressant Tofranil®. After a month, Kim regained enough strength to attend daily group and individual therapy sessions with a psychiatrist. She began to believe some day she would be happy again.

Talking about her feelings with her psychiatrist and the other kids on the ward made Kim feel even better. She learned there were many teenagers who'd experienced the same hopeless depression she had. Within another month, Kim wanted to catch up with the schoolwork she'd missed while depressed. She started attending the hospital high school classes. After a few more weeks, she accepted telephone calls from her old friends and participated in the recreational activities the hospital provided.

With the help of her psychiatrist, Kim began to plan for her return home. And now she was home. She was doing better in school and was again hanging out with her best friend Heather. But she just couldn't feel comfortable around the other kids. Some of them looked at her like she was crazy since she'd been in a psychiatric ward. They didn't know being in the hospital for depression was like being in the hospital for any other illness. In fact, it was better, because once you started feeling better, there were lots of things to do every day.

But now that she was home, Kim felt as if she'd forgotten how to act around other teenagers. Whenever she tried to tell a joke, she muffed the punch line. And she was way behind on the latest gossip, like who was dating whom and which teachers were nerds and which cool. Kim felt particularly left out at lunchtime. Although she sat with a bunch of kids in the cafeteria, listening to their conversations about the hottest rock groups and movies made her feel as if she'd just arrived from Mars.

Kim almost wished she were back at the hospital, where there were kids like her who understood what it was like to be depressed. At least she could still talk about her feelings with her psychiatrist. Kim really counted on her weekly sessions with Dr. Green.

Kim was afraid of how people would treat her at Heather's party. But Heather had made her promise to come, since it was Heather's birthday. Kim sighed, slipped off her headphones, and went to get dressed.

While for some people antidepressants combined with psychotherapy is the most efficient treatment for depression, for others psychotherapy alone is the prescribed treatment. These are people suffering from "situational depression," in which their depression is triggered by a stressful environment or a crisis in life such as the death of a loved one or the loss of a job.

Although antidepressants return chemicals produced in the brain to normal levels, these medications cannot restore a crippled self-image or teach teenagers how to be accepted by classmates. When depression lifts through the use of medication, most people are shoved back into their normal existence, forcing them to confront the wreckage of their lives due to their manic episodes or deep depression. Psychotherapy cushions the shock, helping patients pick up the pieces of their lives.

A depressive episode wastes time—time to be spent in strengthening relationships, advancing academically, and perfecting social skills. When a teenager remains depressed, the normal development process of going from childhood to adulthood is halted. Teenagers need skilled help in order to start the process going again, so they can form peer relationships, achieve independence from the family, and become mentally mature, self-supporting adults.

Most mental health experts believe that without psychotherapy, a depressed teenager will become an adult susceptible to recurring bouts of serious depression.

Robert Hirschfield, a director at NIMH, says, "If the depression is severe, that usually means first prescribing a drug to get the body and mind working in a reasonable way, then looking at the personal problem."[1]

Although like the disease of alcoholism, depressive illness cannot be cured, the combination of antidepressant medication and psychotherapy gets rid of depressed symptoms in 80 percent of the cases.

Some teenagers see psychotherapists on a one-to-one basis, while others attend group therapy with other adolescents, and still others participate in family therapy, in which the teenager and his or her parents, siblings, and significant relatives see the therapist together. How often a teenager sees a psychotherapist depends upon the severity of the depression. Most teenagers see their therapist once a week for an hour.[2]

A psychotherapist may be a psychiatrist, psychologist, social worker, or family counselor. All are trained to help people solve emotional problems. However, only a psychiatrist is qualified to provide both medical and psychological examinations, prescribe antidepressants, monitor the medications, and determine what kind of psychotherapy the person needs.

A psychiatrist is a medical doctor who has attended four years of medical school, and had at least a year of postgraduate general medical study and three years of special training in psychiatry, a total of eight years of medical training.

By contrast, psychologists and social workers are not required to have formal medical training, training in the use of psychotrophic drugs, and do not have to be recertified periodically. In addition, because they are not doctors, they may not prescribe medication. For people suffering from severe depression, with medical and psychological causes, most experts agree that a psychiatrist is the person to see.

Some teenagers hesitate to see any psychotherapist because they think this means they are crazy or weak. They worry that if their classmates or friends find out, they will stop being friends with them, laugh at them, or tease them. But seeing a psychotherapist is not a punishment or something to be ashamed of. It is an opportunity to grow and develop into a more self-confident, capable person.

Therapists who treat adolescents are trained to understand teenage feelings and help teenagers sort out problems and find solutions. A therapist will not tell you how to live your life, but rather will listen to what you are saying, then help *you* make the best choices about how to feel good about yourself, what you want to achieve, and how to realistically go about achieving your goals. The added bonus is that you will have an adult to talk with who will genuinely care about your feelings and help you relieve your depression.

Many teenagers also worry that their therapist will report whatever they say to their parents. Not only does a therapist respect your privacy, but it is a given rule in therapy that whatever you talk about is confidential, no matter how young you are. This means that whatever you say is kept strictly between you and your therapist, no matter what you say about your parents or anyone else. Even if your parents ask your therapist what you said, your therapist will not tell them without your permission.

The only time a therapist breaks this rule of confidentiality is if your situation is life-threatening. If you say you're thinking about killing yourself, your psychiatrist would be obligated to warn your parents about your suicidal thoughts. Or if you are abusing alcohol and/or drugs, your psychiatrist might recommend that you enter a substance rehabilitation center. If you refuse to stop taking drugs, there is a good chance you will eventually overdose. Therefore, the therapist would view your situation as life-threatening and would be obligated to inform your parents of your drug abuse.

If psychotherapists did not care about helping their patients get well, they would not have chosen mental health work as their occupation. It is part of their job to be there for you when you need help. The relationship between a patient and therapist

74

usually turns into a mutually caring and trusting one. Talking to a therapist helps people feel better, as many times patients come up with solutions for problems by themselves, just by discussing their problem with a professional.

There will, however, probably be times in therapy when you recognize certain painful truths about yourself, or remember forgotten unpleasant events in your past. For awhile you may feel worse. But old pains have to be uncovered, cried out, and talked about before you can fully heal your depression. Your therapist will help you find out what the hidden truths are that form the roots of your depression or fear.[3]

Sometimes the solution involves getting your parents to recognize how their own problems are affecting you. Other times, your depression may be getting worse due to an unresolved external factor, such as a grandparent's death. Perhaps your parents have been reluctant to talk about their own feelings of grief over the death, and as a result you have kept your own sorrow to yourself. In this case, the psychiatrist might ask if you would be willing to have a family therapy session, in which you and your parents could air your feelings, with your psychiatrist serving as a guide and mediator.

## HOW DO YOU FIND
## A PSYCHOTHERAPIST?

Probably the fastest way to find a psychotherapist is to ask your family doctor for the name of a psychiatrist, psychologist, or other mental health worker. Or, if your city has a university, look in the phone book for the number of the university's department of psychiatry and call for a list of referrals. Or telephone your local branch of the American Medical Association and ask for names of psychiatrists in your area. You might even ask your school counselor or nurse for the name of someone.

If you cannot afford to see a psychiatrist, psychologist, or social worker, phone your local Family Services Association of America and ask about low-cost family counseling services available in your area, including information about their teen groups. Many cities have community mental health clinics which are supported by federal and state funds, and which offer psychiatric services on a sliding-scale fee (the fee is based upon one's income).

In addition, several national organizations may be helpful, such as the National Foundation for Depressive Illness (NFDI). Their toll-free number is 1-800-248-4344. The National Depressive and Manic-Depressive Association's central branch gives referrals to local branches which have lists of physicians whom their members have found helpful. Their address is Merchandise Mart, Box 3395, Chicago, Illinois 60654, and their telephone number is (312) 939-2442. (Check Sources of Help at the end of this book for more information.)

If you find yourself deeply depressed and feel you need help immediately, nearly every city has a youth crisis or suicide prevention hotline staffed with trained volunteers or mental health professionals. Telephone numbers are usually listed at the front of the phone directory or can be found by asking operator information.

When more studies are done comparing the different types of psychotherapies, there may be a time when there will be a set of guidelines that will tell you the right type of therapy for your type of depression. Until that time, the key to selection of proper treatment is correct diagnosis of the type of depression you are suffering from. And because we are all unique individuals, ultimately the right therapy is what works best for you.

There are no miracle cures for depression, but the combined efforts of psychiatrists, research scientists, and pharmacologists are developing more and more powerful ways to treat this illness.

## TYPES OF PSYCHOTHERAPY

For all kinds of depression, the psychodynamic type of psychotherapy based upon the theories of Austrian neurologist Sigmund Freud is the most widely used. This psychotherapy emphasizes understanding unconscious motivations that make us act in certain ways, and the childhood origins of our present problems.

Psychodynamic therapy includes both psychoanalysis, in which the patient does most of the talking while the therapist sits out of the patient's view taking notes and giving a few prompts here and there if the patient gets stuck; and more intimate psychotherapy, in which the patient and psychiatrist actively talk *to* each other. The length of time a patient remains in psychodynamic therapy depends upon the severity of the depression and underlying problems.[4]

In the 1980s, new, short-term psychotherapies for depression were developed using cognitive (thinking) or behavioral approaches. These new therapies are based upon psychiatrist B. F. Skinner's theories of accenting the present, rather than the past. They operate on the premise that depression itself, not the patient's basic character, should be the primary target of treatment. The new therapies emphasize teaching patients how to behave in ways that help give them more rewarding experiences and feelings.

One of the best known of these short-term therapies is cognitive therapy, developed by psychiatrist Aaron Beck of the University of Pennsylvania. Cognitive therapy works to change patients' negative views of themselves and their world by proving to the patients that their negative views, when examined closely, are not true. Dr. Beck views depressed patients as people who learned inappropriate ways of interpreting their experiences. He believes that with training, these misinterpretations can be unlearned.

A straight-A high school student insisted she was doing poorly in school. Rather than examining her past or trying to change her personality, the cognitive therapist tried to correct her untrue negative ideas and the behavior these negative ideas caused.[5]

In Dr. Beck's twelve-week treatment program, patients are given exercises to reinforce favorable perceptions of even their smallest actions. Dr. Beck also uses behavioral techniques designed to correct three thought distortions characteristic of depressed people: seeing themselves as deficient and unworthy; seeing the world as frustrating and unfulfilling; and seeing the future as hopeless. A 1977 study showed that cognitive therapy was more effective than the tricyclic drug Tofranil® in relieving symptoms and lowering relapse rates in chronically depressed and suicidal patients.[6]

Another form of short term therapy called Interpersonal Psychotherapy (IPT) was developed by psychiatrist Gerald Klerman of Harvard University and epidemiologist Myrna Weissman of Yale University. IPT, consisting of twelve to sixteen weekly sessions of individual psychotherapy, focuses on the present, specifically the patients' problems in relating to others they care about. Based upon the assumption that depression occurs in the context of relations between people, the IPT handbook says, "The aim here is to help patients recognize their complex, mixed feelings of anger, fear and sadness, and devise strategies for handling them."[7]

IPT helps depressed people relate better to those who matter to them by teaching them ways to communicate better with those people, and by challenging the truth of the patient's negative perceptions about these relationships. IPT focuses on each patient's particular problem area, such as extended grief, arguments between teenagers and parents, and major life changes.

In a four-month trial comparing IPT with the tricyclic drug amitriptyline, the drug proved more effective in relieving the physical symptoms of acute depression, such as loss of appetite and energy, while IPT worked better in improving mood and interests.[8]

Two promising group therapies for depression are those developed by psychologist Lynn Rehm at the University of Houston and by psychologist Peter Lewinsohn at the University of Oregon. Rehm's approach focuses on problems of self-management, or the way people organize their behavior to achieve long-term goals. Depressed people, Rehm believes, focus on negative events. They judge their behavior harshly and take the blame for failures, but take no credit for successes. Her therapy trains people to evaluate and reward their behavior more realistically. Meeting for six-to-twelve weekly hour and a half sessions, patients monitor their negative thoughts, make their goals more realistic, give self-praise and blame more accurately, and reward themselves for things done right.

The short-term group treatment developed by Lewinsohn focuses on the passive nature of depressed people that makes them try less and thus receive less rewarding experiences. His treatment is often referred to as the "pleasant-activities" approach, since its methods try to get patients to increase their pleasant activities. Lewinsohn's techniques have been developed into a twelve-session course known as the "Coping with Depression" course. It includes a textbook, *Control Your Depression,* and a workbook.

Another form of short-term individual therapy, based on Lewinsohn's theories and on Joseph Wolpe's assertiveness training, has been developed by psychologist Michel Hersen at the University of Pittsburgh. Hersen assumes that depressed people behave in ways that make others dislike and reject them. Her twelve-session individual therapy treatment helps patients identify the social skills they lack, such as dealing with strangers, friends, and family, and then uses role-playing to teach them new social skills. Patients are also taught when, where, and how to make certain responses to different situations. In a recent study, Hersen found that her therapy was as effective as comparable amounts of dynamic psychotherapy, or the antidepressant amitriptyline.[9]

Besides these new short-term psychotherapies, other treatments for depression have recently been discovered. One was stumbled upon accidentally. A nurse suffering from depression was suddenly switched to the night shift without a break to get some sleep before she started her new hours—from 11:00 P.M. until 7:00 A.M. By the time she ended her shift, she felt 100 percent less depressed.

Researchers in depression at the National Institute of Mental Health heard about her experience. They tried keeping an entire group of depressed people awake all night. By morning, these

79

people were filled with energy, were talkative, and were in a considerably happier mood. "It is remarkable to observe," says Dr. Thomas Wehr, NIMH's chief of psychobiology. "You see someone who has been depressed for a year or two, and within hours, it's gone."[10]

When the researchers found that the patients relapsed into depression when allowed to sleep again, more experiments in sleep reduction with depressed people were conducted. As a result, scientists discovered the important role the body's daily rhythms (also referred to as people's "biological clocks") of wakefulness and energy and drowsiness and lack of energy play in determining a person's mood.

Normally the body's biological clock rises through the day, begins falling with darkness, and starts to rise again just before dawn. Depressed people's biological clocks are out of synch. Their body rhythms move toward wakefulness about 2 or 3 A.M. (the typical early morning awakening found in depressed people). Researchers in sleep therapy, such as those at the Sleep-Wake Disorders Center at Montefiore Medical Center in New York, are trying to reset depressed people's biological clocks to match nondepressed people's biosystems. Some patients who have abnormal night-day cycles in their biological clocks respond well to repeated partial sleep reduction; others respond better to shifting their sleep cycles to correspond with their low periods.[11]

Most people use cues from light and clocks to adapt their schedules to a twenty-four-hour day. "But in some patients—mostly adolescents—the ordinary cues just aren't enough," says psychologist Paul Glovinsky, a sleep expert at Montefiore. "The result is someone who can't function in synch with a normal day, and as a result may become progressively more depressed."[12]

Christopher, sixteen, was referred to Montefiore by a psychiatrist because of his worsening depression. Once an honor student and star athlete, he now fell asleep in class, frustrating himself and angering his teachers. He had lost his enthusiasm for sports and talked about suicide. His sleep habits had changed from going to sleep at 11 P.M. to being unable to fall asleep until 3 A.M.

Doctors at Montefiore put him on a twenty-seven-hour day for a week, in effect resetting his biological clock. The first night Christopher went to bed at 3 A.M. and was awakened at 10:30 A.M.; the following day he went to bed at 6 A.M. and was awakened at 12:30 P.M. Within a week, he had been moved back to a falling-asleep time of 11 P.M. His fatigue and depression soon vanished and he started doing well at school again. The Montefiore team has treated other depressed teenagers suffering from Christopher's "delayed sleep syndrome." Most patients report great improvement in their moods.[13]

Dr. Wehr's researchers at NIMH believe that lack of sleep effects hormone levels. They are investigating the hormonal aspect of sleep, particularly the role of the thyroid-stimulating hormone, a substance that is too low in some depressed people at night, but rises to normal levels, along with mood, after sleep deprivation.

Another discovery about why depressed people suffer from insomnia and early morning wakefulness has to do with when Rapid Eye Movements (REM) occur in normal sleep. REM periods are when dreaming occurs. Nondepressed people usually have the most REM activity during the last third of the night, whereas depressed people usually have the most REM activity during the first third of the night. In sleep labs across the country, scientists can use differences in REM periods to determine whether a person is clinically depressed or suffering from a masked depression such as Alzheimer's disease.

The positive results of sleep deprivation have been found to be caused not by lack of sleep itself, but by the elimination of REM periods that not sleeping accomplishes. Unfortunately, the effect of sleep deprivation lasts only a few days; frequently, though, that is all the time needed before an antidepressant medication begins to work and takes over the job of lessening depression.

Equally useful is a sleep-monitoring technique that can predict whether a particular antidepressant medication will work. If the antidepressant is working, REM patterns move closer to normal within two nights. One sleep lab expert says, "This can save you precious time—weeks in fact—on a medication that isn't going to help a person."[14]

Sleep research ties in with studies of Seasonal Affective Disorder (SAD), first identified by Dr. Norman Rosenthal, chief of outpatient services at the Clinical Psychobiology Branch at NIMH. Scientists have long known that light affects animal behavior (as in determining when animals hibernate). Now they know that light also affects human behavior.

In 1980, Dr. Rosenthal and a team of researchers at NIMH found how SAD might be triggered. They discovered that the pineal gland, a tiny protuberance at the base of the brain, is not a vestigial organ (leftover from human's lower state of evolvement) like the appendix. Rather, the pineal gland is the body's "Dracula" gland. Coming to life each night, it secretes melatonin, a hormone that seems to play a key role in maintaining the biological clock that keeps our body rhythms running on a regular daily cycle of sleeping and being awake. Taken orally, the hormone makes people drowsy, drained of energy. NIMH researchers proved that light lessens melatonin production.[15]

SAD patients who become depressed in winter are being treated with artificial solar light therapy that in effect lengthens their exposure to daylight. The light therapy consists of exposure to a two-by-four-foot rectangular fixture studded with special fluorescent lights that include all the colors found in natural daylight. The fixture produces 2500 lux—slightly less than the light outside when the sun is over the horizon on a clear day. By comparison, the standard fluorescent light in an office is 500 lux. Those who respond to light therapy do so within four days.[16] Light therapy has two drawbacks: the special fluorescent light fixture is expensive, costing from $500 and up; and the light pushes manic-depressive people into a manic episode, in which they become agitated and grandiose.

Because sleep manipulation and light therapy can reduce depression in some patients, have no side effects, and work quickly, these techniques may point the way to a new class of antidepressant devices. One of these may be exercise. There is a constant overlap between body chemistry and mood. After noticing that he "very rarely treated a depressed person who was physically fit," Robert S. Brown, a clinical psychiatrist at the University of Virginia, tested that observation by monitoring the effects of moderate aerobic exercise on ten thousand people. When these people showed a marked improvement in their psychological state, Dr. Brown incorporated an aerobic regimen into his treatment of depressed patients.[17]

# 7
# ELECTROCONVULSIVE THERAPY (ECT)

A nineteen-year-old girl, asleep with anesthesia, lies on a treatment table in a small, brightly painted room in a hospital. Her scalp is wreathed with tiny electrodes that look like she's set her hair with hot rollers. The only sound in the room is the low thump of monitors tracking her vital signs. As a psychiatrist applies a small electric current to her temples, her legs and arms jerk slightly. The electrodes are removed, and she is wheeled into a recovery cubicle in the next room. There she awakens and, although still slightly groggy from the anesthesia, eagerly asks what's for breakfast. The entire procedure has taken no more than five minutes.

This teenager has just undergone ECT, electroconvulsive therapy. Today the application of ECT is light-years away from the tortuous and callously applied "shock treatment" first practiced late in the 1930s on poor, helpless mental patients, regardless of what mental illness they were suffering from.

Although seldom used for anyone under eighteen, ECT is being more widely used for suicidal or homicidal depressed patients,

patients whose physical condition will not allow them to take antidepressants safely, or for the 10 to 20 percent of depressed people who do not respond to antidepressants. In a study of almost 6,000 patients treated with ECT, improvement occurred in about 72 percent.[1] Overall, ECT helps 70 to 80 percent of people with major depression, including those who get relief from medication.[2]

First used in 1938 by Italian psychiatrists, ECT is the oldest effective treatment for severe mania and depression. Shock therapy has had a frightening reputation in the past, much of it deserved. ECT was originally used as a matter of course for mental patients, both as a curative treatment and as a punishment for violent patients who would not follow the rules of the mental institution, where most patients with mental illnesses were housed in the early part of the twentieth century.[3]

The first people treated with ECT were schizophrenics. At that time psychiatrists wrongly believed that schizophrenia was rare in epileptics, and therefore epileptic seizures protected against schizophrenia. As a consequence, thousands of schizophrenics were treated with ECT unnecessarily.

In the past, electrodes were placed on each temple of a patient's head, while the patient was fully awake, and high-energy currents of electricity were shot between the electrodes. Patients had to be tied down, as their bodies went into violent convulsions in the form of a grand mal seizure, similar to an epileptic seizure. Patients' bodies would jerk violently, and they often suffered severe injuries from the violence of the seizures. Their vertebrae snapped, bones broke, and frequently their hearts stopped beating.

Adding to the fearful reputation of ECT was the fact that in the past, a patient's consent to the treatment was not necessary, and anyone on the staff, from nurses to orderlies to doctors, could order that a patient be given ECT. Moreover, not only could the hospital staff force a patient to undergo electroshock treatments, but the staff could give as many treatments as they believed the patient's behavior warranted. Some patients were given fifty or more brain seizures during a single course of treatment, as compared to about six to ten seizures in an entire course of treatment today. The brains of patients in the past, especially their memories, were permanently impaired.

Even if administered to patients who needed ECT, the shock given was so strong that often after these treatments, the patient suffered considerable memory loss for at least two weeks. A woman would be discharged from the hospital, her depression greatly improved by ECT. Yet she might ask her husband which cabinet the dinner plates were in, as she could not remember where she kept things in her own kitchen.

In modern electroshock therapy, the first, and one of the most important, changes is that in order for ECT to be prescribed, the patient must give consent for the treatment. And even then, the patient must be evaluated by three independent psychiatrists, and all three must agree that ECT is indicated before the electroshock therapy can be administered. If these prerequisites are met, the patient undergoes a series of ECT treatments, usually given three times a week on alternate days. The average number of treatments is four to eight, but in some cases, doctors prescribe six to twelve treatments.[4]

Electroshock therapy has several advantages over other treatments. ECT relieves depression rapidly, sometimes after only a single treatment, so patients can more quickly return to normal, productive lives. It has a higher success rate for severe depression than any other single treatment, and it is the treatment of choice by most psychiatrists when a person has been making suicide attempts, as these attempts usually stop after a course of ECT has been started.

In psychotic depression, in which a person has lost touch with reality and has delusions or hallucinations, ECT is more effective than antidepressant medications. With psychotic depression, the medications must be given in higher doses than normal and often in combination with antipsychotic drugs in order to achieve a less prompt, although equally effective, result.[5]

As in any procedure involving the use of a general anesthetic, on the night before an ECT treatment, the person may not eat anything, in order to prevent the possibility of vomiting food during the treatment. And the person is asked to remove dentures, glasses, contact lenses, hairpins, or glass eyes. About thirty minutes before ECT is scheduled to begin, the person is given a drug called atropine, which dries up secretions in the respiratory tract.

The patient lies on a treatment table and a doctor injects a muscle relaxant and a short-acting anesthetic into the patient's vein, putting the patient to sleep. The patient is entirely unaware of the procedure from start to finish and feels absolutely no pain. After the patient is asleep, a rubber mouthpiece is inserted in the mouth to ensure a good breathing airway, and the patient is given oxygen from a face mask placed over the nose. Electrodes are placed on the patient's temples with electrode jelly to help pass electrical contact into the brain.

Then a brief, low-energy electrical current is administered, which passes through the electrodes. The "shock" to the brain causes only a mild convulsion, or seizure, lasting thirty seconds or less. This convulsion consists of a light fluttering of the arms and legs or facial muscles. Only a fraction of the current goes into the brain itself; most of the current is deflected by the skull. Thus, the low-voltage shock makes the convulsion lighter; the muscle relaxants reduce the patient's nervousness and prevent violent muscle jerking; and the anesthesia eliminates any pain.

Patients' brain waves are monitored, as are their heart rates, pulse, and breathing throughout the procedure. Since muscle relaxants can interfere with breathing, following the convulsion, an anesthesiologist releases oxygen through the face mask. Patients usually begin breathing on their own within fifty to eighty seconds after the convulsion.

The entire procedure takes about five minutes, after which the patient, now fully awake, rests for a while and then goes home. While a series of treatments will jolt the depression out of the patient within two weeks, a marked uplifting of mood can be seen much sooner in many patients. Psychiatrists say there is nothing more striking than seeing an acutely depressed patient who, after only two or three ECT treatments, is able to function normally.

An example is the case of the woman who only minutes before her first ECT treatment was sobbing, wringing her hands, and wishing she were dead. Immediately upon awakening from the anesthesia, she smiled and asked what she could have to eat. She even made jokes with the hospital staff.

The major known side effects of ECT are confusion lasting from thirty minutes to an hour after treatment, and memory loss of events occurring six months before and two months after treatment. Memory loss increases with the number and frequency of treatments, but can be lessened by having the treatments further apart, only once or twice a week, for example. A new technique called "brief-pulse ECT" substantially reduces memory loss over a course of treatment by using the minimum amount of electricity needed to produce the convulsion (about one-third as strong as the standard dose.)[6]

Memory loss and confusion can also be lessened by placing the electrodes only on one side of the head (unilaterally), rather than on both sides of the head (bilaterally). In fact, in unilateral treatments there is often no significant confusion at all. Whether unilateral or bilateral ECT is given depends upon the preferences of the patient's physician. In some cases, memory is improved after ECT, probably because the illness of depression itself causes memory loss.

Contrary to popular fears associated with ECT, there is no evidence of learning disabilities or brain damage caused by electroshock therapy. And the risks of physiological damage, such as broken bones, now is very low due to the minimal electrical shocks given.

In 1987, researchers studying the before and after effects of electroshock therapy on the brain were able to use a new technology, the magnetic resonance imaging (MRI) machine, which provides a three-dimensional picture of structures throughout the brain. Researchers found no changes in the brain structure of patients who completed a course of ECT.

According to psychiatrists John H. Greist and James W. Jefferson of the University of Wisconsin Medical School in Madison, Wisconsin, once patients learn the effectiveness and safety of ECT, they often prefer electroshock therapy to any other treatment for depression.[7]

Each year, between 60,000 to 100,000 people are treated with ECT.[8] The drawback is that ECT is not a permanent cure for depression. Patients who improve with ECT, particularly those with a history of recurrent depression, are likely to relapse unless they take some form of medication or psychotherapy following ECT.

In spite of this drawback, however, ECT can be life-saving. Based on a review of patient records at a hospital in Iowa, researchers found that among patients suffering from major depression who were untreated, more than 10 percent died within three years. Although many deaths were due to suicide, 75 percent were due to illnesses such as heart attacks and cancer. Among patients who received ECT, only 2 percent died within three years.[9]

The one specific condition in which physicians believe ECT should not be used is with people who have brain tumors. In one study, patients with brain tumors who were given ECT developed mental or physical deterioration afterwards; in rare cases, lasting brain damage has occurred. People with unusual or severe heart, respiratory, or skeletal diseases are also considered at high risk for a serious side effect from ECT, but these conditions do not necessarily rule out electroshock therapy for these people. Patients with these medical conditions usually tolerate ECT well, and with fewer complications than when treated with antidepressants.

Pregnancy does not rule out the treatment either. Neither is old age a factor in determining who should receive electroshock therapy. In one case, an eighty-four-year-old woman with diabetes and a weak heart was also severely depressed and agitated. The agitation made her heart failure worse, and her life was in danger. Though in poor physical condition, she tolerated and responded promptly to three ECT treatments on successive days. Relieved of her depression and agitation, she paid more attention to taking care of her heart and diabetic problems, and her health improved considerably.[10]

The exact manner in which ECT works to eliminate mania and depression is not known. Studies on animals suggest that ECT, like antidepressants, alters the same malfunctioning brain chemicals such as norepinephrine and serotonin. Most physicians believe the improvement is dependent on producing a convulsion to literally "jolt" the person out of the depressed mood. One study used photostimulation to induce the convulsion in patients rather than electrical shock. The results appeared to be equally successful, indicating that the convulsion, not the electrical shock, is the key to eliminating the depression.

Psychiatrists at the University of Arizona linked ECT's antidepressant effect to an increase in the patient's levels of beta endorphin, one of the body's natural "opiates" produced in the brain to combat pain and stress. Researcher John Misiaszek says he thinks the increased beta endorphin acts to make patients feel better. He believes more knowledge about the range of biochemical and physiological changes caused by ECT might make it possible in the future to substitute neurochemical treatments for ECT.[11]

In countless studies of depressed patients, ECT has been found to work faster to relieve symptoms of depression than any other treatment. Today ECT is no longer the torture depicted in movies like "One Flew Over The Cuckoo's Nest," but rather a painless, effective treatment that enables a severely depressed person to achieve relief from overwhelming sadness and resume a normal life. In fact, some patients with severe depression who have tried both ECT and antidepressant medications said ECT was the most effective treatment.[12]

Yet in spite of proof of ECT's effectiveness in treating depression, a controversy over its use remains. One reason may be the fact that ECT is used for psychological disorders as opposed to strictly medical illnesses. Psychiatrists rightly ask if there would be as much outcry against its use if ECT were used for a more socially acceptable life-threatening neurological illness such as Parkinson's disease, which causes tremors and weakness in muscles.

Another reason for the controversy may be that ECT is done

to, rather than by, patients. When doctors prescribe medication, people take it themselves. In ECT, however, one person does something to another—passes electricity into the brain of the other person.[13]

Despite the controversy, however, until a fast-acting antidepressant is developed, ECT remains the most effective emergency treatment for suicidal, severely depressed, or delusional patients. ECT is also the most fast-acting treatment for depression. In a study of patients who had not been helped by drugs or psychotherapy, 95 percent responded to ECT within six weeks.

With such improvements as briefer electrical-pulse currents and "brain mapping" computers that monitor the currents and direct the shocks to only one side of the head to reduce risks of memory loss, ECT has become, according to one patient who underwent seven treatments and suffered no memory loss, "less painful than dental work."[14]

# 8
# DEPRESSION AND SUICIDE: A TRAGIC AND UNNECESSARY SOLUTION

Mark was sixteen, bright, handsome, athletic. He played the guitar and sang in a band he'd formed with a bunch of his high school friends. Although he'd drink a beer or two at a party, he'd never taken drugs or been in any trouble with the police. He had great plans to become an attorney like his dad. The only times his parents worried about him were on those occasions when he became moody and locked himself in his room.

His moody periods started out happening only about once or twice a month. Then in April of his sophomore year in high school, Mark started spending almost every day alone in his room listening to rock albums. He lost interest in his own band. Although he'd always been a good student, he stopped studying, and his grades fell to Cs and Ds. The day he was scheduled to take his PSAT, Mark overslept, arriving only minutes before the test started. He left many of the test questions unanswered and scored way below his ability.

His parents tried to talk to him, but Mark became so irritable they gave up. They were trying to find a therapist for him, when suddenly he seemed to snap out of his unexplained depressed mood. He started studying again and rejoined his rock band. His parents assumed Mark had just been going through typical teenage blues.

On the Saturday night before Mark's seventeenth birthday, his band was supposed to play at a party in the neighborhood. That day Mark had cleaned his room, mowed the yard, and helped his mother prepare dinner. Afterward, he went to his room. But instead of getting dressed for the party, Mark put on headphones, shoved a Grateful Dead tape into his stereo, turned out the lights, and shot himself in the head with his father's hunting rifle.

Mark's death served no purpose, certainly not for him or his grief-stricken parents. Yet an estimated 400,000 teenagers in the United States unsuccessfully attempt suicide each year, and 5,000 young people actually succeed.[1] Suicide is the second leading cause of death in young people in the fifteen-to-twenty-four age group.[2]

People with depressive illness who commit suicide are not necessarily responding to personal problems with others. Rather, they want to die because their depressive symptoms make them believe they are worthless people. The tragedy is that suicide is a totally unnecessary solution to depression. For when symptoms of depression go away, people who have had suicidal thoughts no longer want to kill themselves and are extremely relieved they didn't act on their suicidal thoughts.

In a study conducted at the Washington Psychological Center, Dr. Alan Berman found that teenagers who attempt suicide share certain characteristics. "Some had parents who were suicidal or who had committed suicide," says Dr. Berman. . . . "Their suicides may have taught the child that if things get rough, this is one way you can handle the situation. If there is a history of suicide in the family, the child may be frightened about his own suicide being predestined. . . ."[3]

Dr. Berman adds, "Most [of these teenagers] had an inordinate amount of stress within the preceding twelve months and a home broken by divorce, remarriage or marital discord. They also tended to . . . have more third adults brought into their world to function in a parental role, suggesting that the third parent was needed because the first two weren't doing too well. The child often becomes attached to the grandparent [or other parental figure] and suffers a huge loss if that grandparent [or other parental figure] dies. We also found a great incidence of parental drug and alcohol abuse among suicidal teenagers and a great deal of anger in these young people."[4]

Dr. Frank E. Crumley, a Dallas child psychiatrist, reported that his patients who had attempted suicide reacted severely to loss and had poorly controlled rage. Most attempted to relieve their depressed feelings with alcohol or drugs, and 40 percent had attempted suicide before.[5]

In other studies of attempted teenage suicides, it has been found that poor communication within the family, a sense of isolation, feelings of rejection, and lack of self-esteem contributed to the attempted suicide. Many of these teenagers had failed to win parental love.

In today's busy, often fragmented family, it is hard for teenagers to fit into a traditional family unit, which adds to their sense of isolation. Most teenagers have a great need to be important to someone else, and when they feel they are not important to their families, they often search for importance in a romantic relationship. The loss of a boyfriend or girlfriend, added to a sense of isolation and rejection, may be the last straw that sends teenagers into suicidal thoughts that all too frequently become actions.[6]

A tragic story is twelve-year-old Vivienne's, who felt a great loss when her favorite teacher moved to another state. She wrote in her diary: "When will I die? It seems like I ought to die now while . . . life has still got some joy." It was her first hint of suicidal thoughts, but no one paid attention. Two years later, Vivienne hanged herself from a water pipe in the basement. Her story is told in the book, *Vivienne, The Life and Suicide of An Adolescent Girl,* by John E. Mack and Holly Hickler.

Some teenagers cannot seem to break the cycle of isolation

and hopelessness. "What many suicidal young people have in common," says Dr. Michael Peck of the Institute for Studies of Destructive Behavior, "is the inability or lack of opportunity to express their unhappiness. They find that their efforts to express their feelings of unhappiness . . . may be ignored. . . . This response often drives the child into further isolation, reinforced by the feeling that something is terribly wrong with him."[7] Yet most teenagers really do not want to die. They want to escape their unhappiness.

Other teenagers believe that killing themselves is a way to get back at their parents or a boyfriend or girlfriend for not caring enough about them or for committing some "wrong" against them. Such teenagers think, "I'll kill myself, and then they'll be sorry for the rest of their lives that they didn't do such and such."

Yes, they will be sorry, but only until the grief and shock run their course. For the truth is that after a period of mourning, if parents or boyfriends and girlfriends let their real emotions come out, the feeling of grief becomes intense rage at the person who committed suicide. As one mother whose daughter took her life said, "How dare she put me through such horror and sadness. I loved her. Killing herself was like a slap in my face. She couldn't have cared about my feelings for her if she made it so I'd never see her again." In countless interviews with people who have lost loved ones to suicide, they say that although the rage lessens into anger, the anger never goes away.

There are no shrines built for people who commit suicide, and there is nothing heroic about suicide. In fact, suicide is taking the coward's way out, as it takes much more courage to fight to work through painful illnesses such as depression than it does to give up and kill yourself. Unlike terminal cancer, depression is not a death warrant. True, it can be an excruciatingly painful illness, but depression is a treatable illness. The key is finding the right treatment for you, and then fighting hard to stick with the treatment until your depression lifts.

The main diagnosis associated with suicide is depression. The second most frequent diagnosis for suicide is alcoholism. Since depressed people frequently abuse alcohol, the primary cause of some of these alcohol-related suicides is depression.[8]

The old belief that people who talk about committing suicide rarely do so is not true. Thoughts of suicide are a common symptom of depression, and people who are really considering taking their lives will often share their thoughts with others.

Treatment for suicide attempters is usually individual psychotherapy or family therapy. Occasionally hospitalization is the only way to prevent these people from committing suicide. Prevention is the main goal in coping with teen suicide. The purpose of the Youth Suicide National Center in Washington, D.C., is to bring suicide prevention into the classrooms. The center's director, Charlotte Ross, says that over 90 percent of suicidal kids turn to their friends for help. The center tries to find experts to go into the schools and teach kids the warning signs of suicide that they can spot in their own classmates.[9]

Some advice these experts give to friends of teenagers contemplating suicide is: If you're not sure whether your friend is thinking about suicide, ask. Don't just say nothing and hope the problem will go away. Don't give insincere advice such as, "Keep your chin up," "Hang in there, you'll make it," or "Lighten up and quit feeling sorry for yourself. We all have problems." But do *listen*. And be honest. If your friend's words or actions scare you, say so. If you don't know what to say, admit it.

Share feelings. Sharing your own "down" experiences makes the other person feel less alone. Get help. If your friend still sounds suicidal, give him or her the number of—or phone yourself—a suicide-prevention hotline. Don't give up until the threat of suicide is gone. If you cannot help your friend, then tell someone else—the friend's parents, your teachers, school principal, nurse, counselor, or other professional. Telling someone else about your friend's wanting to commit suicide isn't snitching. It could very well be saving your friend's life.

Some facts about teenage suicide include the following:

1. More than eight out of ten children who threaten suicide attempt it.
2. The only age group in the United States with a constantly rising death rate is the 15-to-24-year-old age group, and suicide is the fastest-growing cause.
3. Forty percent of teenagers who attempt suicide are drug and/or alcohol abusers.
4. Two-thirds of suicidal young people report poor relationships with their parents. Ninety percent say their parents don't understand them.

In addition, there are forms of behavior that can warn you that a friend is thinking about suicide. These warning signs include:

1. increased sadness, tearfulness, moodiness, or irritability
2. withdrawal from favorite activities and relationships
3. drug or alcohol abuse
4. dramatic changes in sleeping and eating habits
5. an uncaring attitude about clothes and appearance
6. failure in school subjects
7. a preoccupation with death and dying (a fifteen-year-old girl was reading *Death Be Not Proud,* John Gunther's account of his teenager son's experience with brain cancer the night she overdosed on sleeping pills)
8. giving away favorite possessions, such as expensive Compact Disc (CD) cassettes, clothes, or mementos

Relatives and friends often hesitate to bring up the subject of suicide with a family member who is depressed. They hesitate because they fear either that talking about suicide with the depressed person will only upset them more, perhaps even make them violent, or saying it aloud might actually influence them to commit the act.

About 68 percent of people with serious depression openly talk about the fact that they are suicidal. And usually they are relieved that someone cares enough about them to try to talk them out of it. In many cases, talking about suicidal thoughts to someone who cares is a way to stop the thoughts, and thus the action.

Another misconception about suicide is that when a depressed teenager begins to feel better, there is no longer any need to talk about suicide with him. Many teenagers who have had previous thoughts of suicide do indeed kill themselves *not* when they are at their lowest, but rather when they start to feel better.

If you ever feel the urge to take your own life, place an emergency phone call to your therapist, if you are seeing one. If you're not seeing someone, phone a suicide hotline—hotlines can usually be found in the first few pages of the telephone directory—or phone operator information for the number of a suicide hotline. Or telephone the psychiatric unit at a local hospital and ask for someone to talk to about your feelings. Or phone your family physician, if you have a good relationship with that doctor.

Everyone feels better when someone hears them out. Sometimes just talking about your feelings with someone you care about helps you feel like you want to give life another chance. Remember, you can't get a second chance if you're dead. In case after case, when people recover from their depressive episodes, they stop having suicidal thoughts.

If you have had suicidal thoughts or have even attempted suicide, when your depression lifts, you might want to make a list of all the reasons why you want to go on living, such as to be around the people you love, to go to college and fulfill your career goals, to do something you've always wanted to do, such as visit a foreign country, learn how to skydive, surf, or play the guitar. Also write down how the people who care about you would have felt if you had killed yourself. Carry this list with you at all times.

Then the next time you sink into a depression that makes you want to kill yourself, first phone one of the help sources mentioned above. If the hotline is busy or you have to wait while your doctor's answering service notifies your doctor to phone you, take out your list and read it out loud, over and over again, until you start talking to the person you telephoned.

Many teenagers have said that when all else fails and all they want to do is die, what has saved their lives is crying it out. By crying, they do not mean normal, soft sobbing. They mean actually wailing, screaming, and crying so hard they can hardly breathe.

Susan, a fifteen-year-old, said,

> Feeling depressed is like your body is a giant glass with sadness constantly pouring in. When the sadness reaches the top, it just stays there. It won't spill out. That's when you hurt so bad you want to die. You think, "If I killed myself, I wouldn't have to feel this pain anymore." For me, the only way to get the sadness to spill out of the cup is to cry it out.
>
> I use what I call my crying towel. It's a big beach towel. I go into the bathroom, shut the door, and turn on the water in the sink full blast. Then I sit on my knees on the floor, bury my head in the towel, and let it all come out. I mean, really come out. I cry like a baby, loud. Nobody can hear me because the water and the towel cover up all the noise. Sometimes I cry for a half-hour, sometimes for an hour or more.
>
> Afterwards, I always feel better. I don't mean the depression goes away and I feel happy. I just mean that I can deal with the pain again. When you're depressed, the cup is always filled with sadness, but if you can keep it from reaching the top, you can get a handle on dealing with the hurt.

Like Susan, if you can pull yourself up, even just back into your original depression, chances are good that you will believe there is a solution somewhere to your hopelessness, and there will be a time in the future when you will not feel that life is not worth living. As someone once said, "Suicide is a permanent solution to a temporary problem."[10]

# 9
# COMMON QUESTIONS
# ABOUT DEPRESSION

Because depressive illness has many different symptoms and treatments, and not everyone experiences the same symptoms, nor does the same treatment work for everyone, knowing what to do if you have depressive illness can be confusing and frustrating. Here are some of the most often asked questions about depression.

## WHICH TREATMENT IS BEST
## FOR DEPRESSION?

Since depression is caused by different reasons, there is no single best treatment. The best treatment is the treatment which stops *your* depression. However, because it is often difficult or impossible to find the exact cause of a person's depression, the first treatment is usually an antidepressant medication. For until the depression lifts, most people cannot concentrate well enough and do not have the energy it takes to work with a psychiatrist or other therapist to identify and begin correcting the psychological or external causes that have led to their depression.

However, psychotherapy is definitely a necessary and worthwhile treatment once the antidepressant begins working. Most patients with moderate depression and all patients with severe depression need antidepressants as well as psychotherapy. In recent studies of people with moderate depression, a combination of antidepressants and psychotherapy was more helpful than either treatment alone. Moreover, psychotherapy offers the understanding and support everyone needs in difficult times and can help you make changes in your life that can reduce the chances of more depressive episodes.

In addition, some people's bodies cannot tolerate any antidepressant medicine, while for other people, no antidepressant seems to work. For these people, other treatments, such as psychotherapy, ECT, exercise, and sleep deprivation, may be the approach that gives them the most benefit. Only you and your doctor can determine what treatment is best for you.

## DOES HAVING TO TAKE ANTIDEPRESSANTS MEAN YOU ARE MENTALLY ILL OR A WEAK PERSON?

Not at all. Depression is a medical illness, just as diabetes and a bacterial infection are medical illnesses. People suffering from depression take antidepressant medications to help control their extreme sadness, just as people with diabetes take insulin to control their low blood sugar and people suffering from a bacterial infection take antibiotic medications.

If you are unhappy because of something in your life that would make anyone unhappy, then antidepressants will not make you happy. If physical pain is due to a problem other than depression, antidepressants will rarely relieve the pain. These medications work only when the medical illness of depression is present.

101

## ARE ANTIDEPRESSANTS LIKE "UPPERS"?

Definitely not. "Uppers," or pep pills, give you a sudden burst of energy whether you are depressed or not. Pep pills are addictive and dangerous to your body. Antidepressants do not lift an undepressed person's mood. Neither do they make a depressed person suddenly feel high. Antidepressants work on the chemical imbalances in a depressed person's brain to bring them out of depression and into a more normal mood.

## WHICH ANTIDEPRESSANT WORKS BEST?

There is not one single antidepressant that has been proven to work with everyone every time. If you have unipolar depression, you will probably start on one of the tricyclic antidepressants first. Which tricyclic depends upon the opinion of your doctor, after evaluating your particular type of depression—its causes and your medical and psychological history. If you have bipolar (manic-depressive) depression, you will probably be given lithium, which has been proven most effective in relieving or eliminating manic symptoms.

## WHAT IF THE FIRST ANTIDEPRESSANT
## DOESN'T WORK?

Because all antidepressants work on different aspects of chemical imbalances in the brain, there is no guarantee that the first antidepressant you try will work. After a reasonable time, usually six weeks, if you are not feeling any relief from the first antidepressant, your doctor will start you on another tricyclic.

If tricyclic medications do not help your case of depression, your doctor may decide to start you on one of the monoamine oxidase inhibitors (MAOs). Many people who get no relief from tricyclics find that one of the MAO inhibitors is just the right medication for them. An MAO inhibitor is not usually the first medication of choice, simply because of the strict dietary regulations that must be maintained when using MAOs.

## CAN I STOP THE ANTIDEPRESSANT
## AS SOON AS I FEEL BETTER?

No. Antidepressants help relieve the symptoms of depression until the depression runs its course. Since a typical depressive episode lasts from a few weeks to many months, you would be likely to have a relapse into depression if you stopped your antidepressant before your doctor felt you were ready to discontinue it.

## WHAT HAPPENS IF I FORGET TO
## TAKE MY ANTIDEPRESSANT?

Missing one dose is not likely to make you feel depressed again, but repeatedly missing doses can cause a return of depression. If you are taking several doses each day and forget one dose, add it to your evening dose. If you take all your medication in the evening and forget to take it one night, do not try to make up the missed dose by taking the medication the next morning. Just be sure to remember to take your correct dose the following evening. But always be sure to check with your doctor first. Doubling your dose in a single day might cause dangerous side effects.

## HOW LONG DO I HAVE TO
## TAKE THE ANTIDEPRESSANT?

The length of time varies with each person. Your doctor will decide when you should discontinue the antidepressant, based in part on the frequency of your depressive episodes in the past. In addition, your doctor may have you take the Dexamethasone

Suppression Test, to see the level of the antidepressant and other neurotransmitters, such as serotonin, in your blood. With the results of the DST test, your doctor can usually tell whether the chemical imbalances in your brain have evened out enough for you to discontinue the antidepressant.

## HOW WILL AN ANTIDEPRESSANT MEDICATION MAKE ME FEEL?

The main effect of antidepressants is to lift your depressed mood to a normal mood, and prevent a return of depression as long as they are taken. If the antidepressant is working, you should feel less sad, worried, or anxious, and be able to sleep better.

## HOW BAD ARE THE SIDE EFFECTS OF ANTIDEPRESSANTS?

Some side effects, such as dry mouth, constipation, blurred vision, or weight gain, while annoying, are bearable, and seem to lessen or disappear the longer you remain on the medication. By seeing your doctor regularly, any serious side effects can be discovered and corrected. Sometimes these side effects can be eliminated merely by changing the dose of the medication, or by changing the hour you take it. Other times, a change to another antidepressant medication is advised.

## ARE THERE ANY LONG-TERM SIDE EFFECTS OF ANTIDEPRESSANTS?

Tricyclics and MAO inhibitors have shown no long-term side effects, even with people who have taken them for years. Lithium, however, has been shown to cause underactivity of the thyroid gland (hypothyroidism) and a reduction in kidney function in a few patients. Both of these conditions can be identified by routine blood tests and can be corrected.

## DO I HAVE TO BE ON A SPECIAL DIET?

With tricyclic antidepressants and lithium, the only dietary caution is the use of alcohol and street drugs. The combination of tricyclics or lithium with even one alcoholic drink, for example, will have the effect of two or three drinks. If you are on an MAO inhibitor, alcohol may not be consumed, as well as the other dietary restrictions listed in Chapter Five. In general, if you are on a diet that restricts salt or fluids, your doctor probably will not prescribe lithium, as it is a form of salt.

## CAN I EXERCISE WHILE ON ANTIDEPRESSANT DRUGS?

Yes. Exercise is an important factor in everyone's health and has been shown to cause some relief of depression.

## CAN I TAKE OTHER MEDICATIONS WHILE ON ANTIDEPRESSANTS?

Some medications may interact with antidepressants to cause serious side effects. Be sure to tell any doctor you see that you are taking an antidepressant. And before taking any prescription drug or over-the-counter medication, ask your doctor or pharmacist whether you can safely take the other medication while on your antidepressant.

## ARE ANTIDEPRESSANTS ADDICTIVE?

No. Antidepressants are not dope. If you stop taking an antidepressant, you will not have a craving for the medication. However, as with any medication that affects the central nervous system, it is wise to taper off the medication gradually so that your body has time to adjust to the change.

## WHAT IF I NEED TO HAVE
## AN OPERATION WHILE TAKING
## ANTIDEPRESSANTS?

When undergoing any medical or surgical procedure, always tell the doctor involved that you are taking an antidepressant. Do not assume that being on an antidepressant is only important to the doctor who prescribes it to you. A surgeon or other doctor performing a medical test may want you to discontinue the medication for a period of time before the surgery or medical test.

And be sure to tell your psychiatrist or doctor who prescribed the antidepressant about any medical procedures you are going to have. He or she will need to tell you how to taper off the antidepressant and how long it will take until the antidepressant is completely out of your system, so that the surgery or other procedure can be performed safely. In addition, your psychiatrist or other therapist may wish to consult with the surgeon or doctor performing the medical procedure.

## DOES TAKING VITAMINS
## HELP DEPRESSION?

There is no evidence that vitamin or mineral supplements are helpful in treating depression. However, it is safe to take both antidepressants and vitamin supplements. In some rare cases, vitamin $B^6$ deficiency may be a factor in causing depression, usually in women taking oral contraceptives. In this case, supplements of vitamin $B^6$ are important. Occasionally, other vitamin deficiencies, such as vitamin $B^{12}$ deficiency, which causes anemia, can be associated with depression.

106

## WHAT CAN I DO BESIDES TAKE ANTIDEPRESSANTS AND SEE A PSYCHOTHERAPIST TO HELP GET RID OF MY DEPRESSION?

Understanding why you feel depressed is the first step in learning to cope with depression. Depressive illness is sometimes caused by genetic or biochemical imbalances, and at other times by stressful external life events. The three most common feelings in someone who is depressed are sadness, anger, and guilt.

Dr. Marilyn Mehr, coordinator of behavioral services for adolescents at Children's Hospital in Los Angeles, California, says, "Some depressions are bottled-up rage, anger that's gone inward."[1] You might be angry because you are treated like a baby by your parents when you want more freedom; or you are outraged by unfair pressures and demands from your teachers. Rather than express your angry feelings, you hold them in. The result is depression." Dr. Mehr says, "You have to get in touch with what or whom you're angry at and let that anger out. That does not mean physically hurting the other person, but it does mean talking to or even yelling at them if you have to, then taking out your anger by hitting a pillow, for example."[2]

Here are some other ways to pull yourself out of depression *along with* antidepressants and psychotherapy:

1. *Exercise.* Depression is a slowing-down process, so try to speed up your pace. Researchers have found that aerobic type exercises, such as cycling, swimming, running, jogging, brisk walking, or other repetitive and sustained activities that increase your heart rate, circulation, and oxygen intake can actually relieve some of a person's depression. This is because aerobic type exercises cause certain chemicals to be released in your body, such as serotonin, that uplift people's moods. No matter how low you feel, try to force yourself to exercise for at least twenty minutes a day.

2. *Be with other people.* Sometimes just being around others helps relieve depression. Try to focus your attention on another person. Not only will you make that other person feel happy, but you may lift yourself out of your own down mood.

3. *Write in a journal or diary.* Often writing your depressed feelings down on paper makes you feel better, lets you see your problems more clearly, and helps you think of solutions you had not thought of before. Try a two-sided conversation on paper between the strong you and the depressed you. Let these two sides of you battle it out verbally.

4. *Stay away from escape routes like drugs and alcohol.* Drugs like cocaine and alcohol are depressants and addictive and will only send you into deeper depression, besides doing serious damage to your body.

5. *Try to understand what is making you unhappy.* Then avoid the people, places, and activities that make you feel bad about yourself.

6. *Listen to music.* Researchers have found that listening to music can change a person's mood. They call this the "iso-moodic principle." First you match the music to your existing mood; then gradually change the music to match the mood you want to feel. For example, if you're feeling sad, begin by listening to three or four pieces of music you consider sad. Then gradually change them to "happier" pieces of music.

7. *Eat right.* Scientists have found a link between food and mood. Carbohydrates are a sort of "comfort food" because they stimulate the brain's production of serotonin, which makes people feel more calm and relaxed. One and one-half ounces are enough to produce a calming effect, and low-calorie carbohydrates, such as popcorn and pretzels, are just as effective as the more fattening ones, like doughnuts and potato chips. In addition, eating protein sustains mental energy and alertness. The best proteins are found in fish, chicken, veal, and lean beef. Three to four ounces can bring about a calming effect.

8. *Think positive.* Don't put yourself down—for anything. Peo-

ple are often depressed when they think negative thoughts. A study of college students at Northern Illinois University who had recently experienced anxiety or depression found that those students who tried to find something funny about their problems felt better in the long run than those who had just moped around.[3]

Try to recognize when you are thinking negatively and learn to change your down attitude in midthought to a more positive attitude. For example, you look at yourself in the mirror and immediately start to think of all your faults: "I'm too fat, my face is all broken out, my hair is ugly." As you're in the middle of your second put-down . . . "my face is . . ."—*stop*. And say, "My face is pretty (or handsome)." Even if you think otherwise.

Now start saying out loud all the good things about yourself. "I'm a good person. I have a good sense of humor. My hair is a pretty shade of brown. I am a good friend. I have friends. I am honest. I like the shape of my nose, the color of my eyes. I will beat this depression. I can be anything I choose to be."

If you say these positive statements often enough, you will start to believe them. And the positive side of you will take over from the negative side.

Because the earlier depression is diagnosed and treated, the easier the illness is to treat, the Council for Mood Disorders, Inc., a national nonprofit organization based in New York City, has been formed to provide information to the public about depression. In addition, organizations for depressed people are being established, such as Depressives Anonymous in New York City, patterned after Alcoholics Anonymous, in which people with depression meet weekly. This sharing of feelings and experiences helps depressed people feel they are not alone in their sadness, that many other people have been through the torture of despair they have.

There is little doubt that treatments for depression will continue to advance. No one claims to have all the answers. The causes can't always be known, not everyone responds to treatment, and all treatments have their limitations. But the future of the majority of depressed people will be a brighter one. As Jack Barchas, director of the behavioral neurochemistry lab at Stanford School of Medicine, says, "In the twenty-first century, when a patient develops . . . depression, she'll be talked with, tested for a genetic marker, have her spinal fluid analyzed to gauge her brain chemistry, and maybe have a brain scan. From these data will come the vital information on how to treat her individual depression."[4]

Curing depression will not erase all the problems in your life. But proper treatment will give you the means to deal constructively with your problems, using all your capabilities. Now that depression has been recognized as a treatable illness, not an incurable insanity, and now that advancements have been made in psychotherapy and antidepressant medications, there is no reason for anyone to endure the mental anguish and unbearable fear that are the hallmarks of depression—one of the most debilitating diseases known to medicine.

While these treatments do not cure depression any more than insulin cures diabetes, the hope remains that with better understanding of the biological and psychological defects underlying depression, real cures—possibly even prevention—may someday be available. Remember that your situation is not hopeless. Most depressions run their course in time. Try hard not to think of your depression as an endless, dark tunnel. For with the right treatment, there is a light at the end of that tunnel.

# GLOSSARY

*Atypical depression.* A type of depression that cannot be classified as either a major affective disorder, cyclothymic disorder, or dysthmic disorder; seriously depressed patients who do not have the classic signs of depression, such as early morning awakening and loss of appetite, but are chronically unhappy and may even sleep too much rather than too little; a mixture of depressive symptoms and anxiety, phobias, and hysterical features

*Bipolar depression.* One of the two types of major affective disorders, in which episodes of both mania and depression occur

*Cyclothymic disorder.* One of the two types of other specific disorders, in which a chronic disturbance in mood occurs, involving many periods of depression and hypomania. These depressions and hypomanias are not of sufficient severity or duration to be considered a major affective disorder

*Delusions.* Fixed false ideas

*Distractibility.* Inability to keep one's mind on a single idea or object

*Dysthymic disorder.* One of the two types of other specific affective disorders, in which depression is not of sufficient severity to be considered a major affective disorder; often there are normal periods between depression, lasting from a few days to a few weeks

*Endogenous depression.* A depression thought to be due to biological factors that manifests itself by severe depressive symptoms as well as by occasional delusions and hallucinations; when severe, the person is unable to function in a normal social situation; frequently hospitalization is required

*Grandiosity.* A feeling that one has unusual powers or talents, or is descended from an important person

*Hypomania.* Mild mania

*Major affective disorder.* A mood disorder that may either take the form of bipolar disorder (manic-depression) or major depression (unipolar depression); no other psychiatric illness predates the mania or the depression; the mania or depression is considered the major mood disorder.

*Major depression (unipolar).* One of the two types of major affective disorders, which occurs in the absence of any history of mania, and may occur as a single episode or as multiple episodes of depression; major depression is characterized by depressive mood and loss of interest or pleasure in usual activities; this depression is severe, relatively persistent, and associated with such symptoms as appetite disturbance, weight loss, sleep problems, agitation, retardation, decreased energy, feelings of worthlessness or guilt, trouble concentrating, and thoughts of death or suicide, or suicide attempts

*Manic episode, or mania.* A mood disorder characterized by either an unusually elevated or unusually irritable mood, accompanied by hyperactivity, racing thoughts, over-talkativeness, overactivity, distractibility, grandiosity, and financial extravagance

*Neurotic depression.* A depression of varying severity, though usually not severe, in an individual who has had a disturbed personal life up to the time that he or she became depressed

*Reactive depression.* A depression of mild to moderate severity that is a response to a difficult life stress

*Reactive depressive psychosis.* Serious depression or excitement associated with difficult life events and manifested by depressive symptoms as well as delusions and hallucinations

*Retardation.* A slowing down of speech or movement

*Schizophrenia.* A chronic illness manifesting itself by delusions, hallucinations, bizarre thoughts, feelings of paranoia, a blunting of feeling, or inappropriate responses to ordinary stimuli, such as conversation, sights, and sounds; other symptoms are ideas that are expressed incoherently and marked withdrawal from ordinary social events

*Secondary depression.* A depression which occurs in the context of another psychiatric illness, such as anxiety neurosis, alcoholism, or schizophrenia; depressive symptoms are similar to major depression, but occur after the onset of another illness; may also occur along with a serious medical illness

# SOURCE NOTES

*CHAPTER ONE*

1. McCoy, Kathleen. *Coping With Teenage Depression: A Parents' Guide.* New York: New American Library, 1982; p. 7.
2. *Ibid.*, p. 3.
3. Jackson, Stanley W., M.D. *Melancholia And Depression: From Hippocratic Times to Modern Times.* New Haven: Yale University Press, 1986; p. 6.
4. *Ibid.*, p. 7.
5. *Discover*, May 1986, p. 68.
6. Winokur, George. *Depression: The Facts.* New York: Oxford University Press, 1981; p. 28.
7. Greist, John H., M.D. and Jefferson, James W., M.D. *Depression And Its Treatment.* New York: Warner Books, 1984; p. 4.
8. *Newsweek*, May 4, 1987, p. 48.
9. *Woman's Day*, June 1983, p. 66.
10. *Newsweek*, May 4, 1987, p. 57.
11. *Ibid.*, p. 57.
12. *Depression: The Facts*, p. 4.
13. *New York*, June 2, 1986, p. 33.
14. *Coping With Teenage Depression*, pp. 8–9.

15. *Depression: The Facts*, p. 75.
16. *Ibid.*, pp. 73–74.
17. Ketterman, Grace. *Depression Hits Every Family*. Nashville: Thomas Nelson Publishers, 1988; p. 74.
18. Gold, Mark S., M.D. *The Good News About Depression: Cures And Treatments in The New Age of Psychiatry*. New York: Random House, 1986; p. 50.
19. *Ibid.*, p. 51.
20. *Depression: The Facts*, pp. 4–10.
21. *Ibid.*, p. 11.

*CHAPTER TWO*

1. *U.S. News & World Report*, January 24, 1983, p. 40.
2. *Newsweek*, May 4, 1987, p. 51.
3. *Mademoiselle*, May 1986, p. 239.
4. *Discover*, May 1986, pp. 56–57.
5. Klein, Donald F., M.D. and Wender, Paul H., M.D. *Do You Have Depressive Illness?: How To Tell, What To Do*. New York: New American Library, 1988; p. 56.
6. *Better Homes and Gardens*, April 1982, p. 23.
7. *Science*, March 6, 1987, p. 1139.
8. *Science News*, January 28, 1984, p. 58.
9. *Discover*, May 1986, p. 72.
10. *Better Homes and Gardens*, April 1982, p. 23.
11. *Discover*, May 1986, p. 70.
12. *Ibid.*, p. 70.
13. *Ibid.*, p. 67.
14. *Ibid.*, p. 73.
15. *Mademoiselle*, May 1986, p. 239.
16. *Newsweek*, May 4, 1987, p. 51.
17. *Teen*, September 1982, p. 97.
18. *Harpers Bazaar*, June 1983, p. 118.
19. *Discover*, May 1986, p. 73.
20. *Better Homes and Gardens*, April 1982, p. 25.
21. *Science News*, January 24, 1981, p. 58.
22. *Health*, November 1983, p. 8.

*CHAPTER THREE*

1. *Depression And Its Treatment*, p. 92.
2. *New York*, June 2, 1986, p. 34.
3. *Depression And Its Treatment*, p. 97.
4. *Discover*, May 1986, p. 75.

5. *Ibid.*, p. 75.
6. *Depression And Its Treatment*, p. 98.
7. *Ibid.*, p. 99.
8. *Better Homes and Gardens*, April 1982, p. 24.
9. *Depression And Its Treatment*, p. 93.
10. *Ibid.*, p. 94.
11. *Woman's Day*, June 7, 1983, p. 72.
12. *Discover*, May 1986, p. 75.
13. *Depression And Its Treatment*, p. 109.
14. *Mademoiselle*, May 1986, p. 187.
15. *Depression And Its Treatment*, p. 106.
16. *Ibid.*, p. 110.
17. *New York*, June 2, 1986, p. 34.
18. *Depression And Its Treatment*, p. 110.
19. *Better Homes and Gardens*, April 1982, p. 24.
20. *Newsweek*, May 4, 1987, p. 54.
21. *New York*, June 2, 1986, p. 34.
22. *Ibid.*, p. 35.
23. *Chatelaine*, August 1984, p. 33.
24. *Teen*, September 1982, p. 8.
25. *Teen*, February 2, 1980, p. 10.
26. *Chatelaine*, August 1984, p. 33.
27. *The Good News About Depression*, p. 284.
28. *Ibid.*, p. 285.
29. *Depression Hits Every Family*, pp. 61–66.


*CHAPTER FOUR*

1. *Discover*, May 1986, p. 75.
2. *Cosmopolitan*, April 1985, p. 274.
3. *Ibid.*, p. 277.
4. *Discover*, May 1986, p. 75.
5. *Cosmopolitan*, April 1985, p. 277.
6. *Newsweek*, May 4, 1987, p. 53.
7. *Cosmopolitan*, April 1985, p. 277.
8. *Depression: The Facts*, pp. 11–17.
9. *Ibid.*, p. 18.
10. *Discover*, May 1986, p. 75.
11. *Cosmopolitan*, April 1985, p. 276.
12. *Ibid.*, p. 276.
13. *Ibid.*, p. 277.
14. *Ibid.*, p. 278.
15. *Ibid.*, pp. 273–276.

## CHAPTER FIVE

1. Sturgeon, Wina. *Conquering Depression.* New York: Simon & Schuster, 1979; preface, p. *x.*
2. *Depression: The Facts,* pp. 115–116.
3. *New York,* June 2, 1986, p. 42.
4. *Do You Have Depressive Illness?,* pp. 64–67.
5. *Ibid.,* p. 68.
6. *Depression And Its Treatment,* p. 47.
7. *Do You Have Depressive Illness?,* pp. 45–47.
8. *Depression And Its Treatment,* pp. 51–52.
9. *Ibid.,* pp. 64–67.
10. *Ibid.,* p. 50.
11. *Do You Have Depressive Illness?,* pp. 70–75.
12. *Depression: The Facts,* p. 121.
13. *Ibid.,* p. 121.
14. *Ibid.,* p. 123.
15. *Depression And Its Treatment,* pp. 55–59.
16. *New York,* June 2, 1986, pp. 52–55.
17. *Discover,* May 1986, p. 70.
18. *Ibid.,* p. 72.

## CHAPTER SIX

1. *Discover,* May 1986, p. 68.
2. *Woman's Day,* June 7, 1983, p. 72.
3. *Teen,* September 1982, p. 98.
4. *Psychology Today,* June 1985, p. 32.
5. *Discover,* May 1986, p. 76.
6. *Ibid.,* p. 76.
7. *Newsweek,* May 4, 1987, p. 54.
8. *Ibid.,* p. 32.
9. *Ibid.,* p. 56.
10. *Ibid.,* p. 57.
11. *Science News,* January 24, 1983, p. 39.
12. *New York,* June 2, 1986, p. 37.
13. *Ibid.,* p. 37.
14. *Ibid.,* p. 37.
15. *Ibid.,* p. 37.
16. *Ibid.,* p. 36.
17. *Ibid.,* p. 74.

## CHAPTER SEVEN

1. *Depression: The Facts,* p. 130.
2. *Psychology Today,* June 1985, p. 38.

3. *Depression: The Facts*, p. 127.
4. *Discover*, May 1986, p. 70.
5. *Depression And Its Treatment*, p. 63.
6. *Ibid.*, p. 64.
7. *Ibid.*, p. 65.
8. *Newsweek*, May 4, 1987, p. 52.
9. *Psychology Today*, June 1985, p. 38.
10. *Depression And Its Treatment*, p. 64.
11. *Science News*, May 21, 1983, p. 325.
12. *Depression: The Facts*, p. 131.
13. *Psychology Today*, June 1985, p. 40.
14. *Newsweek*, May 4, 1987, p. 52.

*CHAPTER EIGHT*

1. *New York*, June 2, 1986, p. 39.
2. *Coping With Teenage Depression*, p. 252.
3. *Depression: The Facts*, p. 69.
4. *Coping With Teenage Depression*, p. 253.
5. *Ibid.*, p. 253.
6. *Woman's Day*, June 7, 1983, p. 72.
7. *Coping With Teenage Depression*, p. 256.
8. *Depression: The Facts*, pp. 64–67.
9. *New York*, June 2, 1986, p. 39.
10. *The Good News About Depression*, p. 290.

*CHAPTER NINE*

1. *Teen*, February 1980, p. 9.
2. *Ibid.*, p. 9.
3. *Readers' Digest*, January 1989, p. 95.
4. *Discover*, May 1986, p. 76.

# SOURCES OF HELP

*DEPRESSION HOTLINES AND HELP AGENCIES*

• You do *not* have to live in the same state or city of a particular agency in order to use its services.

• If you are in an emergency depressive situation and need to phone an out-of-state agency, but cannot afford to pay the long distance rate, *phone collect.*

*DEPRESSION/SUICIDE HOTLINES:*

The fastest way to get in touch with a depression or suicide hotline in your city is to phone operator information and ask for the number of your local "Suicide/Crisis Intervention Hotline." A "Suicide/Crisis Intervention" phone number is also listed at the beginning of phone directories under "Useful Numbers: Emergencies."

119

*NATIONAL RUNAWAY HOTLINE:*

1-800-621-4000

This hotline offers help and referrals to both runaway shelters and counseling services across the United States.

• NOTE: It may take awhile to reach this hotline, as their number is frequently busy.

This hotline is located at:

The American Association of Suicidology
2459 South Ash Street
Denver, CO 80222


*AGENCIES OFFERING REFERRALS OF PHYSICIANS AND CLINICS FOR DEPRESSION AND INFORMATION ABOUT DEPRESSIVE ILLNESS:*

American Psychiatric Association
1700 18th St., N.W.
Washington, DC 20009
(202) 797-4900

American Psychiatric Association (APA)
Division of Public Affairs
1400 K St., N.W.
Washington, DC 20005
(202) 682-6220

American Psychological Association
1200 17th St., N.W.
Washington, DC 20036
(202) 833-7600

The American Association of
Marriage and Family Therapy
924 W. 9th St.
Upland, CA 91786
(714) 981-0888

(has over 7500 members in the United States and Canada. Write or call for free referrals to qualified family counselors.)

National Youth Work Alliance
1346 Connecticut Ave., N.W.
Washington, DC 20036
(202) 328-3052
(for name of runaway/teen crisis shelter in your area)

National Committee on Youth Suicide Prevention
67 Irving Place South
New York, NY 10003
(212) 532-2400

Depression and Related Affective Disorders Association (DRADA)
Johns Hopkins Hospital, Meyer 4-181
600 North Wolfe Street
Baltimore, MD 21205
(301) 955-4647

Manic Depressive and Depressive Association
222 South Riverside Plaza
Chicago, IL 60606
(312) 993-0066

National Depressive and Manic-Depressive Association (NDMDA)
Merchandise Mart, M-Box 3395
Chicago, IL 60654
(can provide information about depression and reference sources for physicians across the United States)

Depression Awareness, Recognition, and Treatment (DART)
National Institute of Mental Health
Public Inquiries, Dept. G
5600 Fisher Lane, Room 15C-05
Rockville, MD 20857

(provides free books and pamphlets on the causes and treatment of depression)

National Mental Health Association
1021 Prince Street
Alexandria, VA 22314
(703) 684-7722

*FAMILY SERVICES OF AMERICA:*

The Family Service Association of America has agencies in every major city in the United States, and offers low-cost individual and family counseling and special rap groups for teens. Check your telephone book for the office in your area.

# FOR FURTHER READING

Gawain, Shakti. *Creative Visualization.* San Rafael, Calif.: New World Library, 1979.

Gold, Mark S., M.D. *The Good News About Depression: Cures and Treatments in The New Age of Psychiatry.* New York: Random House, 1986.

Greenberg, Hannah. *I Never Promised You a Rose Garden.* New York: Holt, Reinhart, & Winston, 1964.

Greist, John H., M.D., and James W. Jefferson, M.D. *Depression and Its Treatment.* New York: Warner Books, 1984.

Hickley, Holly, and John E. Mack. *Vivienne: The Life and Suicide of An Adolescent Girl.* Boston, Mass.: Little Brown, 1981.

Ketterman, Grace, M.D. *Depression Hits Every Family.* Nashville, Tenn.: Thomas Nelson Publishers, 1988.

Klein, Donald F., M.D., and Paul H. Wender, M.D. *Do You Have Depressive Illness? How to Tell What to Do.* New York: New American Library, 1988.

Kline, Nathan S. *From Sad to Glad.* New York: Ballantine Press, 1981.

Knauth, Percy. *A Season in Hell*. New York: Harper & Row, 1975.

Neufeld, John. *Lisa Bright and Dark*. New York: New American Library, 1969.

Peck, Scott M. *The Road Less Traveled*. New York: Simon & Schuster, Inc., 1978.

Sturgeon, Wina. *Conquering Depression*. New York: Simon & Schuster, Inc., 1979.

# INDEX

126

## ABOUT THE AUTHOR

Herma Silverstein has spent a decade writing, teaching, and lecturing around the country. She is the author of eight books and many stories and articles for children. Ms. Silverstein has written books for young readers on a variety of topics, and especially enjoys the research involved in nonfiction writing. When she's not writing or researching a book, Ms. Silverstein keeps an active schedule of lecturing and teaching. She has been a panel participant for the International Reading Association and a lecturer in the Southern California public schools.

Ms. Silverstein lives in California.